THE FAMILY MANAGER
Saves the Day

THE FAMILY MANAGER
Saves the Day

RESCUE YOUR FAMILY FROM EVERYDAY STRESS
FOR A PEACEFUL, POSITIVE HOME

Kathy Peel

A Perigee Book

A Perigee Book
Published by The Berkley Publishing Group
A division of Penguin Group (USA) Inc.
375 Hudson Street
New York, New York 10014

Perigee trade paperback edition: August 2004

Visit our website at www.penguin.com

Library of Congress Cataloging-in-Publication Data

Peel, Kathy, 1951–
    The family manager saves the day / Kathy Peel.—1st Perigee pbk. ed.
        p. cm.
    ISBN 0-399-53003-7
    1. Mothers—United States—Time management. 2. Child rearing—United States. 3. Work and family—United States. 4. Family—Time management—United States. I. Title.

    HQ759.P429 2004
    640'.43'0852—dc22

                                                                        2004048351

Printed in the United States of America

10 9 8 7 6 5 4 3 2 1

Contents

Acknowledgments

During the course of writing this book, many people saved the day for me. Much love and heartfelt appreciation go to my husband Bill and our three boys, John, Joel, and James. Being your Family Manager for thirty-three years continues to be my greatest joy. I am also deeply grateful to my good friend and agent, Patti Dematteo, and to John Duff and Katie McHugh at Perigee Books.

The Family Manager's Creed

I oversee the most important organization in the world—
Where hundreds of decisions are made daily
Where property and resources are managed
Where health and nutritional needs are determined
Where finances and futures are discussed and debated
Where projects are planned and events are arranged
Where transportation and scheduling are critical
Where team-building is a priority
Where careers begin and end

I am a Family Manager.

Introduction

Being a mom means there's always more than plenty to do—and the job starts over every morning. If we don't find ways to handle day-to-day tasks so that everyone, *Mom included,* is cheerful, relaxed, and organized, we will all struggle just to endure life and never get to enjoy it. How we carry out each twenty-four-hour day can make a difference between a household in constant uproar and one that hums along smoothly. I call this job being a Family Manager.

Why think of yourself as a manager? Because there is more at stake than just lost car keys on Monday morning or a missed school play due to unexpected calendar conflicts. Home is where our kids learn how to "do" life. It's where they see a model of how to run a home, and they'll be sure to emulate our example in their adult lives. Consequently, we need smoothly run homes both for sanity's sake and for our kids' future success.

Today you might be right in the thick of it, wondering if you'll ever have another peaceful moment in your life. If so, I feel your pain. I know what it's like to think a good night's rest is two hours of uninterrupted sleep! Just about everything you feel, I have felt, too: I speak from the experience of more than three decades of marriage and the struggles and delights of raising three boys (now grown). On days when the kids had ball practices at the same time on different sides of town, or when they shared the stomach flu, I remember my mother saying, "These days will pass so fast." I also remember thinking, *Not fast enough*.

The good—no, great—news: As a Family Manager, you have the power to save your family's day. You can bring chaos under control and create a harmonious home. You can make serenity and confidence a lifestyle.

How?

First, by managing time instead of letting it manage you. The trick is figuring out the fastest, most efficient way to tackle the *have to's* so there's more time for the *want to's*. In my estimation, the more *want to's*—reading for pleasure, playing tennis, picnicking, and flying kites as a family, for instance—you can fit into your week, the more fulfilling and balanced your family's life (not to mention your own life) will be. Managing your minutes wisely is the key—and the result is lower stress.

These are hectic times. More than ever families need home to offer rest, renewal, and fun. I'll give you lots of tips for shaping your own time-management style, one that will benefit every person in your family.

Second, by actively managing your family. It seems obvious, but many moms who feel their home is out of control aren't seeing that a home is an organization. In my mind, managing kids can be likened to being your family's Human Resources department. In every company, HR offers opportunities for employees to excel by building their skills. When grievances or disputes arise, HR steps in to resolve them and by offering tangible rewards—bonuses or promotions, for instance—and HR inspires workers to do their best work. In a family, HR is spelled M-O-M.

We need to begin living with an awareness that our vital job as wives, mothers, daughters, and friends is to build loving, lasting relationships. All of us want to know that there are others who care where we are, what we do, and who we become. We all need a retreat from the world—a peaceful place when we are stressed, a warm corridor when it's chilly outside. Such a sanctum is bound together with the strongest glue I know of—family and friends. Family Managers know how to inspire their "staff" and make home a great place to be.

Third, by making celebrations a family affair. As your family's manager, you're likely the one who organizes and coordinates the special events in your family's life. These projects might be small or large, once-in-a-lifetime or annual affairs. They're called "special" because they're important memory makers, ones not to be missed. But like anything else in life that is significant, they take time and work to pull off.

At home as well as the office, planning something big usually requires the help of other people. So if you need some help with pulling off a party, you can share the load. When family members assist with cooking, decorating, running errands, addressing invitations, confirming reservations, and so on, it's a huge load off Mom. That means you can actually take pleasure in the festivity, instead of just being solely responsible for making it happen. Again, when Mom's having a good time, everybody's having a good time.

And last, but certainly not least, by making your own health and contentment a priority. Yes, you read that right. You know the old adage, "If Mama ain't happy, ain't nobody happy." It's true! So a calm, contented family must start with you.

When our own needs go unmet, our bodies get stressed and start reacting. Our minds race in turmoil, our emotions are erratic, and our spirits become discouraged. We are in no condition to nurture anyone else. A good Family Manager has to manage herself first. I'll show you simple, practical ways to make this ideal a reality.

Does this sound like a direction you'd like to take? Are you ready for a new plan— one that works in very tangible ways? Remember, your family does not need a cranky, tired, resentful wife and mom. They need someone who can give freely and guide joyfully because she has resources from which to draw. She has kept her own reservoir full, she knows her management role and how to use it, she controls her own clock, and she shares the workload.

This can be you! Hang in there—what you're doing is very, very important work. Whether you also work full- or part-time in the marketplace, volunteer, or go to school, hear this: At home you're tackling the most valuable tasks imaginable: nurturing lives and running your family—the most vital organization in the world.

Get ready to learn how to do all of that with a lot more ease—and joy. You *can* save your family's day and gain your own peace of mind as well.

Save Time

Running a home and raising a family means there is always plenty to do. Unfortunately, cooking, cleaning, doing laundry, and grocery shopping never seem to take a vacation, and if you're like most moms I know, no one is clamoring to take over these responsibilities for you. After years of dreaming about how much better my life would be if I could only add an hour or two to my day, I finally came up with ideas that worked for me—to manage the twenty-four hours I do have.

I wish I could give you a magic formula for getting it all done in less time with less stress, but there isn't one that works for everyone. But what *does* work is giving some thought to the ages of your kids and their schedules; the amount of time you can devote to keeping up with the house, shopping, and cooking each week; and your personal style. When my kids were young, for instance, I did laundry every day, but I have a friend with four children who lets the dirty clothes accumulate until there's nothing left to wear. At that point she starts the washing machine.

Perhaps you're the type of mom who can't go to bed unless her house is in order for the next day—the kids' lunches are made, the kitchen is tidy, and you have a plan for tomorrow night's meal. Or maybe you're just not a plan-

*

"The future is something which everyone reaches at the rate of sixty minutes an hour, whatever he does, whoever he is."
—C. S. Lewis

ner. You spend the evening relaxing after a long day of working, chasing kids around, or both, and when tomorrow comes, you just wing it.

Whatever your style, there are ways to use time more efficiently, and this section has lots of time-making, stress-reducing ideas. But before you read on, relax. Time, after all, is no more than moments, and all moments are manageable.

Getting in Touch with Your Priorities

Do you ever feel frustrated at the end of the day because projects and people who weren't even on your radar took up time you hadn't planned to spend? Being a mom requires flexibility and guarantees interruptions. In many ways our time is not our own, and that's one of the sacrifices and privileges that comes with being a parent. Children—and life events—are predictably unpredictable. Many things in our hours and our days we cannot control, but some we can. But before we can get a handle on those things, it is imperative that we know what's most important to us.

"Things that matter most must never be at the mercy of things that matter least." —Goethe

This is where knowing our priorities makes such a pivotal difference. Our priorities are made up of both the most theoretical parts of our lives (why we do the things we do) and the nitty-gritty practical parts (what we do and how we do it). Our priorities should reflect *our* values—not those of our best friend, boss, or favorite celebrity.

Too often our priorities are revealed, not chosen. We're frequently too busy to sit down and think about what is most important to us—and the fact is, our family life suffers when this happens. If we don't decide, others will decide for us. To start the process of getting in touch with what you consider vital and time-worthy, consider these questions and answer them as concretely as possible:

1. What things are most important to you: financial security, a fulfilling marriage, a loving relationship with your children, peace of mind, good friends, social status, spiritual fulfillment, a loving extended family, interesting work, travel, education, fun and recreation, a great body, pretty clothes, a nice car, a beautiful home, recognition or fame, good health, longevity?

2. What kinds of issues, needs, and activities motivate you?

3. If you could meet any need in the world and could not fail, what would you do? Is there a group of people or cause you are deeply concerned about?

4. If you won the lottery, how would you spend the money?

5. If you knew you had only a year to live, what would you do?

6. What is your worldview? In other words, how do you answer these life questions: Where did I come from? Why am I here? Where am I going? Does life have any meaning and purpose?

> "Perhaps it would be a good idea, fantastic as it sounds, to muffle every telephone, stop every motor and halt all activity for an hour some day to give people a chance to ponder for a few minutes on what it is all about, why they are living and what they really want."
> —James Truslow Adams

See if there are patterns in your answers. Think about your responses for a day or two, then make a list of your top five priorities. Doing this exercise will help you:

- Clarify what matters most—what you want for your own life and your family's lives.

- Focus your time, energy, and resources.

- Know when to drop activities—and which ones—when you feel overloaded with responsibilities.

- Make decisions based on your own values and priorities.

> "Tell me to what you pay attention, and I will tell you who you are." —Jose Ortega Y Gasset

Now you know why you're doing what you're doing!

Avoid Side Roads and Destructive Distractions

We live in an age of data overload. Every day we're bombarded with information that's intended to help us form our priorities and move us to make decisions. Television and glossy magazine ads make real life seem gray in comparison to their make-believe spotless kitchens, professionally engineered closets, and women still perfectly dressed and coiffed after a long day's work. Twenty-four-hour news channels and newspapers bombard us with current stories on how we live now—or should. There are books on topics our foremothers never even heard of. And the Internet gives us immediate access to information and images from the world over. I'm not saying information *per se* is a bad thing—far from it. I like to know what's happening in the world. I want to learn new things that help me become a wiser, better mother, wife, friend, and professional. But we need to filter all that's thrown at us. There are some things we simply don't need to know.

When we don't think about what's worth thinking, saying, or doing, it's easy to get sidetracked.

A Priority Isn't a Priority Unless You Act on It

Everyone has different priorities, of course, but I imagine that because you're reading this book, you desire to raise good kids, build a strong family, and be sure your home is comfortable, happy, peaceful, and rewarding for everyone who lives there.

The minutes of the day we have with our children come with a choice on how we'll spend them. The same is true for any other priority: The choices we make to act on them determine how strongly we hold them.

"The best things in life aren't things." —Art Buchwald

Our Choices Shout Our Priorities

When business leaders set priorities, they think about those priorities in terms of the impact following them will make. For instance, companies that have a serious commitment to customer satisfaction set return policies, hours of operation, and many more things that reflect that priority. As Family Managers, we live out our priorities in each of the seven departments we oversee in our homes (see the following sidebar), and how we spend our time in each department says a mouthful about what those priorities are.

For example:

"If you let decisions be made for you, you'll be trampled." —Betsy White

HOME AND PROPERTY

Is it more important to have an impressive magazine-cover-worthy family room with expensive furniture and fragile décor? Or do you choose attractive but comfortable furniture that says, "Come on in and sit awhile, prop up your feet, let your hair down, be refreshed"? It depends on your priorities.

FOOD

If eating well without spending hours cooking is high on your priority list, you might create a Favorites folder on your computer for quick links to good, quick-meal-idea websites. Or you might enlist anybody who's big enough to hold a spoon in helping to cook and get dinner on the table, thereby spending time with your children and teaching them responsibility.

FAMILY AND FRIENDS

If working on your marriage is a priority and spending more intimate moments together in the bedroom is one way you're going to do this, then you'll look at your calendar and figure out which nights during the week would be likely ones for a romantic rendezvous after the kids go to bed. You'll look for ways during the days to conserve some energy and think romantic thoughts to get ready.

If taking a class to buff up your computer skills is a priority and attending your son's basketball games is another, you compare your son's sports schedule with those at the community college. You then choose a class at a time that lets you root for your son in person as well as build your skills for the workplace.

The job of Family Manager is much like that of a CEO of a corporation, someone who oversees various departments. Our job description looks something like this:

- **Home and property.** We oversee the maintenance and care of all tangible assets, including personal belongings, the house, and its surroundings.

- **Food.** We efficiently, economically, and creatively meet the daily food and nutrition needs of our family.

- **Special events.** We coordinate large and small projects—holidays, birthdays, vacations—that fall outside the normal family routine.

- **Family and friends.** We deal with family life and relationships as a mother, wife, daughter, sister, friend, teacher, nurse, counselor, mediator, social chairman, etc., as required.

- **Financial.** We budget, manage investments, pay bills, and handle a host of other money issues.

- **Time.** We manage the master family calendar so everyone gets to the right place, at the right time, with the right equipment, and the household runs smoothly.

- **Personal.** We nourish and care for our body, mind, and spirit.

FINANCIAL

Is it a higher priority to have a large nest egg in savings or to spend some of the money to add on a family rec room or go on a fabulous once-in-a-lifetime family vacation? How could you cut costs and still have a good vacation? Is anybody in your family a do-it-yourself-er?—You? Your spouse? Your teenager who got an A in shop? Could that person teach the rest of you a trick or two, and could you re-model for less money while spending time together as a family?

SPECIAL EVENTS

If you prioritize honoring who each of your children is, then do you impose the birthday party you always wanted on your nine-year-old daughter? Or do you let her choose? I have a friend who gave her daughter that very option. The mother worked with her as she painstakingly outlined each idea on paper, thinking of whom to invite, what they would do, and where the party might be. Instead of discouraging her daughter's creativity, her mother talked with her about how much lead time they'd need to execute each party idea, costs, and how to weigh various options and make decisions.

Not only did this girl get to make a choice on her own, thereby learning something about living by her priorities, she also learned a lot about making a plan and executing it. And she learned that her mother cared about her very much. (Visit www.familymanager.com to download and print a free child's party planner.)

TIME

Say you put a premium on spending time with your child. This means you don't raise your hand when your boss asks for volunteers to work at the food bank or when a friend calls needing help to put on a yard sale—because you've promised to take your child to the library for Story Hour. On the other hand, perhaps another of your priorities is teaching your child to be responsible and show compassion for others. Perhaps you say yes to your boss after all and take your child with you.

> ### Deep Pockets Not Necessary
>
> You don't need a lot of money to choose to spend great time with your kids. Going on field trips to state parks, walking the dog and talking about the day, baking cookies together on a rainy weekend afternoon, reading a story together every night without fail—that's the stuff meaningful relationships are made of.

PERSONAL

Which is more valuable: to say yes, you'll work through your lunch hour on a project, or say no, because you have a prior commitment to attend a spin class you signed up for?

Avoiding the "Too Busy" Trap

Maybe you agree that choosing priorities and living by them is a great idea—but you feel too overwhelmed by life to sit down and figure out what's most important to you. Perhaps you're thinking, *I'm so busy I can't even take time to sort them out, let alone live by them.* This is a trap. Don't fall into it.

The fact is, fulfilling your commitments to your family, the office, and the community *are* overwhelming at times. All of us face numerous obstacles that keep us from setting priorities and ordering our lives the way we would like. The big three I had to come to terms with in my own life are:

- **Circumstances.** Unless we stop and decide it's vitally important that we take an hour or so and go someplace quiet, where we can think about what's important to us, the natural course of life will carry us out of control along a path of minimal accomplishments, meaningless activities, frustration, and mediocrity.

- **Expectation and pressure from others.** We are all, more or less, prone to succumb to the agendas of others, appropriate the goals of our culture, and compromise. Let's be honest—peer pressure is not just a teenager's problem. It's a lifelong issue. And it's never too late to start standing on your own and supporting your priorities.

- **Love of the comfortable.** We tend to arrange life as best we can to avoid pain and maintain our personal comfort. The problem is that we experience no significant change for the better, no personal growth, and no relational development without stepping out of the comfort zone. Maybe it's time to sacrifice now for a long-term payoff.

Taking Charge of Your Priorities

Maybe your life is running out of control. You know you haven't been living by the priorities you want to. You know things have to change. What to do? It's time to weave some new ideas into the existing fabric of our lives. We need to alter—sometimes slowly, other times abruptly—and look for ways to incorporate the new tactics, behaviors, and activities into our lives that will produce positive changes.

> "Change is not made without inconvenience, even from better to worse." —Samuel Johnson

This means starting someplace. If you're having trouble beginning with the "small pebbles" to "move the mountain," I suggest that you think about one day at a time. You might even want to get yourself a small notebook in which you write down your top priorities. Then, as you make choices during the day, simply jot down a few words about the choice you made and how it did or did not fit your stated priorities. You're not doing this to beat yourself up for not making choices according to your stated priorities. You're doing it to become conscious of your actions.

If you know what you want to be and do, you must also know what you don't have to be and do

Learning to Say No

I was once where you are. Twenty years ago, I was a busy mother of young children and all that means—practices, lessons, car pools. I said yes to everyone who asked me to volunteer for worthwhile projects in the community and at church; and I also had a part-time business. But after all those "yeses," I finally ended up in the hospital. It's not a pretty picture when Mom crashes and burns. But sometimes it takes a painful experience to teach an important lesson. That was a turning point in my life. I couldn't do everything—instead I had to decide what I valued most in life. I had to begin to make daily decisions about how I spent my time, energy, and resources according to my priorities, which were and are my faith, my family, and my profession, in that order. And that means sometimes choosing to say "No."

Ten Principles of Time Management

Here are my ten time-tested principles for achieving these very satisfying goals:

- **Write it down.** Don't trust things to memory. Using lists and checking off completed tasks frees your mind for more important things. (See "The Daily Hit List," page 12.)

- **Do it now.** Sir Richard Tangye said, "During a very busy life I have often been asked, 'How did you manage to do it all?'"

The answer is simple: it is because I did everything promptly." Make this your motto—especially with onerous tasks that could become worse if you put them off.

- **Have the right tools.** The projects for which we have the tools or resources will be finished before the ones for which we're not prepared. If you schedule some time to organize your child's closet, have on hand various sizes of organizing bins, self-sealing plastic bags, a garbage bag, and boxes to store or give away items.

- **Believe in buffers.** If you think something's going to take you thirty minutes, schedule forty minutes. Anticipate traffic, check-out lines, and children to be slower than you'd like, and adjust your expectations.

- **Set deadlines.** Deadlines are the best guarantee a job will be done. Jot down on your calendar the time or day you want to have a task completed. If need be, ask a friend or family member to hold you accountable.

- **Do advance work—don't wait until the last minute.** If you're hosting a party, decide what you can do a week ahead of time, the day before, and so on. Estimate how much time you'll need and when to schedule tasks; anticipate potential time-wasters. Then set deadlines for accomplishing goals.

- **Work with your biological clock.** If you're a morning person, do your most important work then. Schedule tasks that don't demand as much attention and brain-power during lower-energy times of day.

- **Create boundaries.** Set your priorities, and don't let other people guilt you into crossing them. Give yourself permission to "just say no" to requests

Benefits of Time Management

There is no such thing as unimportant time. Each day is a gift.

Becoming a good manager of time has valuable benefits. You will:

- Spend less time on the things you *have* to do and more time on the things you *want* to do

- Have a sense of fulfillment when the day is done

- Reduce daily stress and keep frustration to a minimum

- Be a model for your kids

- Enjoy a balanced, all-around better life for you and your family that dent time with your family or time spent nourishing yourself. Keep in mind, when you say yes to something, you're saying no to something else.

- **Take charge of your own life and schedule.** Do things on your time: Don't pick up the phone every time it rings—use voicemail or an answering machine. Turn off your "You have mail" alert. Answer when it's convenient for you.

- **Don't wait for time to "free up."** If you have a big project to accomplish, schedule work appointments with yourself in thirty-minute or one-hour blocks. Be serious about this time as you would any other appointment. Before you know, you'll have the project licked.

The Daily Hit List

Do you ever get up in the morning and think, *I've got so much to do I don't know where to start?* In my efforts to live efficiently—to control and not be controlled by the daily needs and demands of my family and career and to plan ahead effectively—I created what I call a Daily Hit List. This is a to-do list that's divided into the seven departments you and I oversee as Family Managers. Just organizing by category will allow you to weigh the importance of various tasks and prioritize. It has saved my sanity and can save yours as well. Using a Daily Hit List will:

- Declutter your mind by providing a systematic way to sort through the myriad chores and responsibilities that crowd in every morning.

- Clear your perspective, revealing what's trivial and what's priority.

- Clarify which tasks only you can do and which can be delegated or shared.

- Improve your memory through the exercise of writing down details.

- Help you remember what steps to take today so whatever's coming tomorrow will be smooth.

- Create a record for future reference of when you did what.

As you begin to use a Daily Hit List, accept the reality that you won't always be able to check off all the tasks on your list at the end of the day. Things come up: Kids get sick (sometimes several at once), the car gets a flat tire on the way to school, your baby-sitter has to cancel. Don't be discouraged! Move unaccomplished tasks to the next day's list, or delete the ones you deem unimportant for now.

There are three steps for making this list work for you:

- **Do.** Think about and list *everything* that needs to be done. This includes obvious things such as meals for the kids, gas for the car, and money in the bank, as well as other responsibilities such as running errands, carpooling, and scheduling appointments.

- **Delegate.** Looking at your list, ask yourself, *What can I delegate?* Can a teenager start a load of laundry before she leaves for school? Can a younger child fold clothes when he gets home from school? Can my husband start dinner when he arrives home from work? Always delegate according to skills, age, and availability—not gender.

- **Delete.** Once you've delegated, take another look at the list. Are some of the tasks really expendable? Do you really need to mop the kitchen floor every day? What is truly unnecessary, at least today?

Visit www.familymanager.com to print off a free Daily Hit List.

Memory Joggers

Every day you deal with countless bits of information. Here are a dozen tips for reminding yourself of something you can't afford to forget. Apply the ones that fit your style.

- Stick a note on the bathroom mirror, your exit door, or the car's steering wheel.

- When you receive schedules for anything from school to soccer to dance class, write the dates and locations *immediately* on your calendar. Use a highlighter to make important events stand out.

"Nine-tenths of wisdom consists of being wise in time."
—Theodore Roosevelt

DATE:

DAILY HIT LIST™

SCHEDULE

5:00
6:00
7:00
8:00
9:00
10:00
11:00
Noon
1:00
2:00
3:00
4:00
5:00
6:00
7:00
8:00
9:00
10:00
11:00
12:00

NOTES

HOME & PROPERTY	FOOD	FAMILY & FRIENDS
MONEY	**SPECIAL EVENTS**	**SELF**

©1999 Family Manager Inc.

- Have a calendar program such as Outlook or the alarm on your PDA or cell phone alert you when you need to remember to leave for a meeting or start the grill for dinner.

- Set your oven timer to remind you to stop cleaning out drawers and leave to pick up the car pool at school.

- Use an alarm clock. It doesn't have to be used just to wake you up in the morning. Set it for a time you need to do something during the day.

- When you're away from home, call your own voicemail or answering machine and leave yourself a message to remember to do something.

- Carry a small notebook in your purse and/or car. Take a minute to write down pertinent information.

- Turn it into a game with your kids. One autumn I was having trouble remembering to shut the garage door when coming home from doing errands. This meant leaves could blow in, causing more work for the boys when they swept it. We put a jar on the counter, and every time I forgot to close the door, I had to deposit a dollar in their jar.

- Keep a spiral notebook near your phone and make notes of phone conversations on the day you have them. It keeps you focused on the call, plus the information and when you obtained it sometimes comes in handy down the road.

- If you are going to a party, write in your planner not only the time of the party, but also the address if you are not familiar with the location. Also list things you need to take somewhere, such as gifts and borrowed items.

- Don't try to keep records in your head. Write down appointments on your family calendar. Keep notepads and pens in convenient locations such as by each phone and on your nightstand. But don't let your data-keeping become paper clutter. Post information on a bulletin board near your Control Central (see the box on page 16), then act on it, file it, or toss it ASAP.

> Write *Reward for Return* and your phone number on the front page of your planner in case you misplace it. Or make a label for your handheld computer that says the same.

■ If you keep your car in a locked garage, put clothes for the dry cleaner and videos to be returned on the driver's seat the night before. You won't be able to miss them when you leave in the morning.

Scheduling Strategies

Traveling to and from and waiting at appointments can eat up hours of valuable time. Sometimes you have no choice when you have to wait in line or for an appointment, but these tips will help you keep travel and wait time to a minimum.

Appointments

■ Try to schedule the first appointment of the day or the first appointment after lunch. It's less likely that you'll have to wait.

■ Call before you leave for an appointment at your hairdresser or doctor's office. If he or she is running late, use the extra time to get something done.

■ When you make an appointment, write the office or person's phone number on your calendar so you won't have to look it up if plans change. If you've never been to the office or location before, get directions when you make the appointment and take the office's phone number with you when you go.

■ Schedule family members' dental check-ups and kids' pediatrician appointments back-to-back so you can make fewer trips.

■ Avoid scheduling "maintenance" check-ups at the doctor or dentist in May, August, or December—the busiest months of the year for moms.

Control Central

Every business manager has a base of operation—a place from which he or she carries out management responsibilities. It's no different for a Family Manager. We need a home base of operation—a place to organize and administrate the countless daily details: activities, appointments, invitations, phone numbers, and school forms, among others.

Be it a desk, countertop, or office, Control Central is the place where you call the shots: track your family's schedule, note changes, respond to messages, make lists, and keep all those important papers in their places. By setting up your own Control Central, you can better oversee your family's comings and goings and manage the countless tasks, responsibilities, and decisions that are made every day. If the CEO is calm and organized, everyone else is, too.

- Schedule kids' back-to-school or summer camp physicals well in advance.

- When you schedule an appointment, if you'll need a baby-sitter, arrange that at the same time.

- Make multiple appointments for the same day. You'll reduce getting-ready and travel time.

> ### Double Benefits
>
> Taking a book, magazine, or newsletter with you wherever you might encounter wait time is a good way to stay sharp mentally—and model the importance of lifelong learning to your child as well.

- Always take your calendar with you to an appointment so you can schedule follow-up visits while you're there. You'll have your pick of the schedule, and you won't forget to write down the new appointment.

- Bring along toys or books for small children.

- If you're running late for an appointment, be courteous and call. Let them know you're on your way and when you'll arrive.

- Many services and businesses now offer online scheduling—a big time-saver.

Making Phone Time Count

The phone can be our best friend or worst enemy. We decide which it will be by determining that the phone will not run our lives but help them. Here are some simple ways to save and use time better on the phone:

- Set your cell phone or pager to vibrate instead of ring. Don't let it interrupt what you're accomplishing at the moment—unless it's a family member.

- Set time limits on your phone calls and take them only at certain times of day. Keep a watch or timer handy. If you make a call and are asked to hold but can't, say no.

- Call service businesses on Thursdays or Fridays. (Their busiest days are Monday and Tuesday.) Call during the slower hours. Companies' busiest periods are from 10 A.M. to 2 P.M. and from 5:30 to 7:30 P.M. Schedule repair calls online whenever possible.

- Get out of the "I must answer the phone when it rings" habit. Let your voicemail or answering machine take calls. Return them when it's convenient for you.

- Consider getting a distinctive, second ring on your phone line. For a minimal monthly charge, your phone company can set up two or more numbers to ring distinctively on one phone line. Give the new number only to family members so you'll know when they're calling.

- Take some time to program the speed-dial features on your home phone and cell phone, if you haven't already done so.

- Purchase a phone with a caller ID feature.

- Cut solicitors short by saying, "Thank you for calling, but I'm not interested. Please take my number off your list."

- Call long-winded friends or family just before lunch or at the end of the day.

- Gently guide nonstop talkers to the point. Remind them you have only five minutes to talk, or schedule a time when you can talk longer.

- Highlight all numbers you look up in the phone book. They'll be easy to find again.

- Create a three-ring family phone book that lists all the numbers you call regularly: services, stores, friends, neighbors, relatives, and so on. Keep one at each phone in your house, in your car, and at the office.

- Use a portable phone or headset so you can walk around while you talk.

- Store a box of stickers, activity books, and small toys by the phone to distract a small child when you have to make an important call.

- Avoid "phone tag" by making appointments for phone calls. Treat these calls the same as you would treat a face-to-face appointment. Put them on your calendar and make notes about what you want to talk about. Think of it as a meeting—it is. Be prepared with any info you need before the call.

Register your phone number on the National Do Not Call Registry. Visit www.donotcall.gov for instructions.

■ When you need to call someone back at a later date, write the name and phone number on the calendar so you won't have to look it up.

■ Use e-mail rather than phone calls. It's often faster.

■ While you're on hold:

Clean out your purse.
Purge your coupon file of outdated coupons.
Organize a drawer.
Dust the closest piece of furniture.
Polish or file your nails.
Straighten your desk.
Clean your glasses.
Tidy your sewing box.
Organize your wallet.
Clean out your jewelry box and untangle necklaces.

Planning Ahead

"Good family management means you have to live in two tenses." When I recently made that statement at a Family Manager seminar, a woman in the audience cried out, "I must be doing a great job, because I'm always too tense!" We all welcomed the comic relief but felt her pain.

It's true. To keep a home and family functioning effectively, a Family Manager has to pay attention to the details and demands of the day but also look ahead to what's coming up on the calendar and take steps to ensure that the right actions will take place at the right time and include the right people with the right equipment at the right location. Whether it's getting your family out the door—shoes tied, zippers zipped, faces free of grape-juice stains—for your cousin's wedding, or researching what you'll need to do to your house to have it ready to put on the market when summer comes, you have to consciously work on today and tomorrow at the same time. By developing a habit of looking ahead on your calendar, thinking about where you're going and what you want to see happen, then mak-

"You've got to think about 'big things' while you're doing small things, so that all the small things go in the right direction."
—Alvin Toffler

ing plans, you'll be ready for anything. Imagine how many headaches you can avoid!

Here are just a few ways you can be "ready for anything":

- Look at your calendar at the first of each month to see what nights you need a baby-sitter. Arrange for them now.

- Keep your list of baby-sitters updated and growing. Ask friends and neighbors for referrals so you have plenty of options if your regular sitter has to cancel. (Keep their contact information in your family phone book, along with the hours they are usually available.)

- Mark your calendar, or have your computer alert you, one month before holidays and birthdays. Begin early to plan celebrations and buy presents and decorations.

- Start planning summer vacations and checking into kids' summer camps in February.

- Schedule a time in the summer to have pictures taken of your kids. Enlarge one to give Grandma and Grandpa for Christmas.

- Plan for fun. Collect information and save some money each month for that trip you want to take for your tenth anniversary three years from now.

- Pick four or five easy dinner menus that you can prepare in less than thirty minutes, and keep the ingredients on hand for those days when you have to stay late at work or don't have time to fix the fajitas you'd planned on.

- Keep take-out menus in a file at work so you can place an order before you leave and pick it up on your way home.

- Have a contingency pick-up plan in place if your son or daughter gets sick suddenly while you're tied up at work.

Smart Move

My lifelong friend Kataryn Waldrep is a busy obstetrician/gynecologist. She keeps an ongoing list of tasks and errands—10-minute, 30-minute, one hour—in her daily planner. When a small block of time opens up she checks her list to get something accomplished toward a future event or deadline.

- After you get your car's oil changed, write the next due date on your calendar. Ditto for getting the tires rotated.

- Be ready for tax season. Start to gather the materials you'll need in January. When a period of time becomes available, you'll be ready.

- Keep an emergency set of clean clothes for your child put away for that day when you have to go someplace and you haven't had a chance to do laundry.

- Keep a change of clothes and/or accessories at the office in case of unplanned meetings or dinner engagements.

- Stock up on office and school supplies so when your child tells you at 9 P.M. he needs a pocket folder for a report due the next day, you're Johnny-on-the-spot.

- If you have small children, stock your car: Keep on hand a diaper bag, dry wipes, wet wipes, a change of clothes for the kids, and plastic containers filled with nonperishable snacks.

- Always have gifts put away on your closet shelf for when your friend's (or your child's friend's) birthday is (*whoops*) today and you've forgotten or your child tells you an hour before the birthday party.

- Stock up on sale items even if you won't need them for a month or two.

- When the winter sales hit, buy your kids' coats (a size bigger) for use next year.

- Keep one-dollar bills and quarters on hand. You never know when you'll need them.

Finding More Time, Getting More Done

Have you come to dread the sight of your to-do list? As a mother whose kids are now grown, I can tell you that the list never gets shorter. (Instead of picking up the kids at school, now I'm picking them up at the airport!) I still have to find the time to cull bulging closets, reorganize drawers, and purge the freezer

> Give family members a heads-up on what is expected of them. If you want your son to mow the lawn on Saturday, don't wait until Saturday morning to make your request.

of UFOs (unidentified frozen objects). The large blocks of time to accomplish these tasks are few and far between, but fortunately, I've discovered a hidden treasure. What treasure is that? Five-minute segments. You'd be surprised how much you can accomplish in 300 little seconds, and how many 5-minute segments you can grab here and there. Granted, you won't finish tasks like unloading the basement of ten years' worth of clutter, but you'll make progress every time you work on it—which will make you feel better about yourself—and eventually the project *will* be finished!

In 5 minutes, you can:

- Purge your pantry of food you never use, one shelf at a time.

- Clean out a portion of your freezer and refrigerator.

- Wipe down kitchen counters and backsplash.

- Reorganize your dish cupboards, one at a time.

- Remove duplicate items from kitchen drawers.

- Sort through a junk drawer.

- Clean out a couple shelves in your medicine cabinet.

"Every minute is a golden one for him who has the vision to recognize it as such."

—Henry Miller

- Declutter a shelf in your linen closet. (Keep two sets of linens for each bed and give away the rest.)

- Sort children's clothing, one drawer or shelf at a time.

- Purge through a basket of magazines and catalogs; toss old ones.

- Remove clutter from one surface area.

- Dust one room.

- Wipe fingerprints off a few doorjambs and light switches.

- Check the batteries in your smoke detector.

- Throw in a load of wash.

- Fold a load of laundry.

- Sew on a button.

- Empty waste cans and take out the trash.

- Vacuum a room.

- Sweep the front porch.

- Water plants.

- Check the air pressure in your tires or check the oil.

- Call to make an appointment.

- Sort mail.

- Pay a few bills.

- Answer an e-mail or two.

- Purge your e-mail inbox or clean up computer files, five minutes at a time.

- Add new contact information to your family phone book.

- Make a Daily Hit List (see page 12).

- Put DVDs or CDs back in their cases.

- Pick up some toys or clutter in your family room.

- Do some crunches, push-ups, and leg lifts.

- Take vitamins and drink a big glass of water.

- Moisturize your face.

- Write a thank you note.

- Pray for friends.

Multitasking Made Easy

Some time-management gurus don't believe in multitasking. They talk about being "present in the moment"—giving something our whole attention. Maybe that's a reaction from people who once wore themselves out trying to do two or more things at once—and trying to give both equal mental focus. Real multitasking is different: It involves doing things that *don't* require a person's full attention. And there are plenty of tasks that don't deserve our full attention!

Doubling up on tasks lets us spend more time on fun and other things to which we want to give our attention. Get started by listing tasks that can be done simultaneously. Post the list in a central location. Every time you "catch" someone multitasking, praise and/or reward him or her! This is a great habit to teach your children.

TWO-TIMING IDEAS

- Never walk through the house empty-handed. Pick up as you go. If you're going upstairs, take something that belongs up there with you.

- Encourage teenagers to start a load of laundry before tackling their homework. When they stop for a snack, they can move the clothes from the washer to the dryer.

- Have kids strip beds and take linens to the washer while you put on new sheets.

- Request that kids fold clothes, sort socks, brush the dog, or reunite a basket of toys with missing parts while they watch cartoons—definitely an activity that does not require full focus!

> "Good words are worth much, and cost little."
> —George Herbert

- Divide and conquer. To get in and out of the mall faster, each person should take a separate list and meet back at a designated time and place.

- Give yourself a manicure while you watch the news.

- Ask young kids to wash patio furniture and bicycles while older ones wash the dog and the car.

- Teach preschoolers to identify colors while they are cleaning, by first picking up the blue toys, then the red, etc.

- Have a meaningful conversation with a child while you walk the dog.

- Clean the bathroom mirror and shine fixtures while tending your child's bath.

- Put away groceries while you talk on the phone.

- Wash dishes or unload the dishwasher while waiting for the water to boil.

- Set the table for the next meal as you unload the dishwasher.

- Make a grocery list while you cook dinner. Check the pantry as you go.

- Have kids swish their hands and feet around the tub during a bubble bath to loosen bathtub ring.

- Before you run errands, consider what else you might pick up or drop off along the way.

- Cook two, three, or four meals at once. Clean carrots for tonight's pot roast, afternoon snacks, and tomorrow night's salad.

- Make soup and stew at the same time. Double the recipe and you'll have tonight's dinner and another for the freezer.

- Read a book or look through catalogs while you're on the exercise bike or step machine. Plan purchases; glean gift ideas.

- Bathe the dog while you water the garden.

- Buy two or three each of household staples—deodorant, shampoo, soap—so you won't have to make a special trip again soon.

- During TV commercials, have everyone pick up and put away clutter.

- Steam wrinkles from clothes by hanging the garment in the bathroom while you shower.

Prescriptions for Procrastinators

At times we all need a jump-start to get us or to keep us going. But if procrastination is a consistent problem for you, try to understand why you put things off. If you fear doing a poor job, remember that doing your best—not achieving perfection—is your true goal. If you think you "thrive under pressure," consider whether the stress you go through defeats doing your best work.

Try one or two of these ideas to help you accomplish a task you've been dreading. Remember, time adds up—24 hours, 1,440 minutes, 84,600 seconds a day—whether we use it or not. A little action now can add up to a big result at the end of the day.

Getting Started

■ Gear up the night before. If you plan to tackle a project one morning, set out the supplies or tools you'll need and the clothes you'll wear. Go to bed a little earlier than usual so you'll wake up refreshed and ready to go.

> "Nothing is so fatiguing as the hanging on of an uncompleted task."
> —William James

■ Make the steps to completing the task tangible. List each step you'll need to accomplish. Breaking the task into smaller segments will help you maintain momentum. As you finish each segment, give yourself the satisfaction of checking it off in red ink!

■ Have the right tools available to tackle the project. If you are going to excavate the clutter in the basement, buy plenty of clear plastic storage bins in various sizes. Save the receipt; you can return the ones you don't use.

■ Ask someone you have fun with to help you with the job.

■ Speed up your metabolism. Before starting the task, take a brisk, twenty-minute walk.

■ Remove distractions from your environment. Turn off the TV, close the door, and turn off the ringer on your phone.

WHILE YOU'RE WORKING

- Do the worst part first. The rest will seem easy!

- Put on some peppy music that makes you want to move.

- Listen to a motivational tape.

- Stop and pat yourself on the back when you finish a segment of the task. If you have six drawers to clean out, congratulate yourself each time you conquer one.

- Ask a friend or family member to monitor your progress and encourage you along the way.

- Start a fifteen-minute rule. Spend fifteen minutes every day on something you've been procrastinating about. Before you know it, you'll have the dreaded task licked.

- Give yourself the freedom to stop and rest if you need to.

- Visualize how you will benefit from finishing.

> Kids are notoriously good at procrastinating. Teach them these strategies to help them tackle a big school project.

REWARD YOURSELF!

- Decide beforehand how you will reward yourself when you complete the job.

- Buy a little something to make the task more pleasant. If you dread spending a day in the kitchen cooking and freezing a week's worth of meals, buy yourself a cheery apron or a new pot you've had your eye on.

- Fix yourself a treat to keep you going. On attic clean-out day, put a plate of enticing fruit on a counter or table near the door leading outside to your garbage cans. When you travel to and from the attic, you can grab a bite.

- Post inspirational quotes in your work area. Read them when your motivation starts to wane.

Creating Routines

Do you find yourself wasting time and energy on the same tasks or refereeing the same arguments day after day? When I was a young mother, I noticed that the same things were frustrating me repeatedly. For example, I regularly lost my car keys and arrived places late, made a lot of unnecessary midnight runs to the drugstore, and left a lot of wet clothes in the washing machine (I wasn't proud my washer had a mildew cycle). These were just three of the things for which I definitely needed to create some standard operating procedures.

If you relate, creating routines will help you reclaim precious minutes and save your last nerve. Hundreds of tasks are required to keep a family going, and many of them can be fitted into routines that make everyone's life easier. Once you decide how, when, and by whom something should be done, you eliminate questions and arguing—and you stop wasting time on the trivial.

Routines allow us to spend time and energy on the important things, like brainstorming the solution to a problem with a child, deciding what we as a family would like to do together this weekend or going to the park to fly a kite with the kids. Routines help replace time-stealers with time itself—that most precious commodity. They free us to stick to our priorities, doing what we truly feel is important and essential, and they give family members security because everyone knows what to expect. Finally, routines allow us to be more flexible and spontaneous because we're not always trying to decide what to do next.

> *"I am working to improve my methods, and every hour I save is an hour added to my life."*
> —Ayn Rand

Routines start with a notepad, a pencil, and a cup of coffee. The following section, "Routines Worth Creating," will help you identify recurring problems in each area you oversee as the Family Manager and their possible solutions. Tackle one or two new routines at a time. Before you know it, you'll realize some issues are no longer sources of conflict, and peace has replaced frustration.

Routines Worth Creating

FOOD

Problem: We never know what we're having for dinner.
Fix certain meals on certain days. Maybe you always
grill hamburgers on Saturday night and have breakfast
for dinner on Sunday night.

> If you get up 30 minutes earlier every
> day for a year, you add seven and
> one-half days of "awake" time to your
> schedule.

Problem: Mom's doing all the work. Create a house rule: The family members who
didn't cook the meal will be responsible for cleaning up.

Problem: We're always running to the store for ingredients. Plan menus ahead and
write down all ingredients needed. Keep your pantry well stocked. Shop in bulk
once a month at a wholesale club. Visit the grocery store weekly for incidentals
during off-peak hours.

What Routines Can Help With

Meal planning	Assisting with/doing homework
Food shopping	Clothes shopping
Cooking and preparing meals	Family finances and bill paying
Cleaning up after meals	Errands
Straightening up the house	Taking clothes to dry cleaners
Vacuuming	Car maintenance
Making beds	Yard work
Doing laundry	Watering plants
Cleaning bathrooms	Pet care
Exercising	Mail and paper clutter
Collecting and putting out trash	Communicating with your spouse
Recycling	Spending quality time with your kids

Problem: We keep running out of dishes. Always start the dishwasher after dinner. Put away dishes and set the table for tomorrow's breakfast before bed. Give yourself the freedom to use paper plates and cups now and then.

Problem: The dishes are so sticky by the time we get to them, they're impossible to clean. Clean dishes immediately after eating. If that's not possible, fill the sink with hot, soapy water and soak the dishes.

Problem: Making the day's lunches in the morning just adds to breakfast chaos. Fix tomorrow's sack lunches while you're cleaning up after dinner.

Problem: Breakfast is always fast and furious (and I do mean **furious***).* Set the table and make as many preparations as you can the night before. Offer a very limited menu of easy-to-prepare but healthful foods. Divide preparation and cleanup chores among family members.

FINANCES

Problem: We tend to let balancing the checkbook go—for several months at a time. Set a time to balance your checkbook soon after you receive your statement. Or use computer software such as Quicken to keep your finances up to date.

Problem: We're paying too many late fees on bills. Pay bills on the first and the fifteenth of the month, or pay them immediately as they come in. Set up as many bills as possible to be paid via automatic draft from your bank account. Many banks allow you to set up automatic payments online.

Problem: We never seem to have cash when we need it, so we're always running to an ATM. Budget how much cash you'll need each week, and go to the ATM once a week for that week's cash. Keep it in an envelope. Have family members write down on the envelope what they take cash for so you can track spending. And designate a certain place to put receipts whenever you make a purchase.

Problem: We religiously clip coupons, but we never seem to see the savings. Get cash refunds when you use coupons, and put the money in a savings account. Many grocery stores have branch banks on the premises. Save for something special.

Problem: We're frequently rushing to the video store at a late hour and paying late fees. Rewind videos immediately after watching, and load DVDs back in the case. Put them on a shelf or in an errand basket by the exit door.

FAMILY AND FRIENDS

Problem: Our schedules are so hectic, it seems we're always in the car on the way to the next practice or appointment. We need to do fun things more often. Start a fun routine with each of your children: getting frozen yogurt together after dance practice, playing a quick game of Ping-Pong when homework is finished, or reading a chapter from a book aloud before bed.

Problem: Homework is a steady source of conflict. We're always fighting about getting it done, and sometimes the kids wait until bedtime to start it. Always do homework right after dinner. And create a no-screen-time-until-homework's-finished rule.

Problem: Morning conversation centers around just getting out the door. I hate to send my kids off on that note. Use breakfast time to encourage your kids and show interest in their worlds. Talk about their day and what's coming up: tests, trips, special projects. (If, however, you're the kind of family who needs to stare at the cereal box for a half-hour without speaking, do that. You can chat more in the evenings.)

Use the last moments together to encourage: As your kids walk out the door, say, "I love you. Have a good day—you're a great kid!"

Problem: The kids fight about chores and who did what last week. Create a morning chore chart so there's no more arguing about whose turn it is to feed the dog or take out the garbage. Post it at kids' eye level. Let younger kids put a sticker next to a task when it's completed. (Visit www.familymanger.com to download and print a morning chore chart.)

Problem: The kids can never find office supplies when they need them: pens that still write, rubber bands, paper clips, etc. Set up a Control Central that includes a mini-home office and ample amount of basic office supplies (see page 16). Purge it regularly of pens that don't work (a good task for kids).

Problem: Getting the kids to help out around the house is more trouble than it's worth. Call a family meeting and create house rules everyone can live with. Have consequences for noncooperation (see House Rules, page 59).

Problem: I'm tired of refereeing between my kids. Make sure your house rules cover things like sharing toys, time spent at the computer, etc.

Problem: The kids or I often forget small items at home and have to make extra trips on school days and workdays. Have children load their backpacks the night before. Put everything you need to take—purse, briefcase, errand items—near the exit door.

HOME AND PROPERTY

Problem: We have a big family and it's hard to keep track of whose sheets I changed and when. Change the sheets on Mondays. Have kids strip the beds as soon as they get up and put linens in the laundry room. Have kids who are old enough help with putting clean sheets back on their beds.

Problem: Newspapers and junk mail pile up for weeks before we get around to dealing with them. Make a policy of putting each day's paper in the recycle bin before you go to bed.

Use cardboard magazine holders to create a family mail center. Personalize a holder for each individual, and have one just for catalogs and magazines. Place a trash can nearby. Toss junk mail immediately as you sort the rest.

Problem: Mom ends up doing all the housework, even though everyone contributes to the mess. Have a rule that kids do not get their privileges—watching TV, playing computer games, talking on the phone—until they fulfill their responsibilities. Stand firm.

Problem: Clutter is making all of us crazy. We can't find the things we need when we need them, and the house looks messy all the time. Create a family policy that says family members are not to put things *down* but to put them *away* after using.

Have a nightly seven-minute sprint. As a

> Don't let what you can't do stop you from what you *can* do. Even small changes can make a big difference.

timer ticks off seven minutes, everyone in the house picks up and puts away the clutter accrued that day, plumps sofa pillows, changes cat litter, and so on.

Create a Clutter Jail. When family members leave out their belongings, put the items in a box or crate. The culprits must post bail before they get them back.

Problem: Everyone loses track of vital items: permission slips, car keys, baseball gloves, etc. Create an inbox for each family member. When kids get home from school, have them unload backpacks right away and put important papers in their inboxes.

Put a hook by your exit door and your keys on it when you walk in the door. And just in case: Always keep an extra key to your house hidden outside and an extra car key in your purse or calendar notebook.

Keep a lost-and-found basket in the front closet. Whenever anyone finds clothing, sports equipment, toys and such lying around, he should stash it there. Family members then know where to start looking for something they've lost.

SPECIAL EVENTS

Problem: We want to celebrate each family member on his or her birthday in a way that makes everyone feels equally special. Start a family birthday routine. Hang curling ribbons from the chandelier and let the honoree choose the menu for dinner. Have each family member state what he or she appreciates about the birthday person.

Problem: Stuff we don't use is piling up everywhere, taking up needed storage space. Have a garage sale after you spring-clean every year. Locate a charity drop-off box that's convenient to your errand-running orbit. Set a goal to donate some items every month.

Problem: We can't afford to go out to dinner once a week, but we need some family time to reconnect. Schedule a family fun night at least twice a month: play games, pop popcorn, etc. Disconnect from the world—turn off cell phones, TV, etc.—and focus on each other.

Problem: Everyone in our neighborhood is so busy—we don't really know each other. Host an annual holiday open house in your neighborhood. Or, organize an annual neighborhood-wide garage sale.

* TIME AND SCHEDULING

Problem: My mom tends to call when I'm at my busiest, and I feel bad having to cut her off. Call your mother at an agreed-upon time every week. You'll both be available and ready to talk.

Problem: I have a hard time saying no to my friends and co-workers, so my schedule gets full and I get stressed. Never agree to a request on the spot. Always check your calendar first. It's okay to say "I'll get back to you."

Problem: I keep forgetting to feed the fish. Feed pets every morning while brewing coffee.

Problem: Ironing is such a drag that I avoid it until the amount is overwhelming. Cut down on ironing: As soon as the clothes are done in the dryer, fold or hang. Teach kids this habit early. Then, iron every week during your favorite TV program.

Problem: I can't seem to exercise regularly. Meet your neighbor for a brisk walk on Monday, Wednesday, and Friday at an agreed-upon time.

Problem: We have a family reunion coming up in a couple months, and I'm overwhelmed by all I need to get done. Every Sunday night, look at the week's calendar. Identify tasks you can accomplish in small bits of time that will help your reunion run more smoothly.

Problem: The kids lag in bed until the last minute, so they're always rushing in the morning. Give each child an alarm clock. Let them suffer the consequences of running late. Don't rescue them!

Problem: Every morning there's a tense line at the bathroom door. Design a rotating schedule for the bathroom, and assign each child a time. Put a timer in the bathroom so they'll know when their time is up. (Teenagers should get up fifteen minutes earlier than younger siblings because they need more time in the bathroom. Put a makeup mirror in girls' bedrooms to free up time for others.)

Problem: The kids seem to get ready for school just at the last minute. Inspire your child by providing a special toy or game to be played with only when he is ready a few minutes early.

Create a no-play-until-ready rule.

Keep distractions to a minimum. Leave the TV off unless a child needs to watch a news report for a class.

Problem: I find myself spending too much time on my hair and makeup every morning. Find a hairstylist who's an expert at cutting hair, and get a good cut that's easy to manage. Ask him or her to show you how to style your hair. Keep a clock or timer near the mirror where you apply your makeup. (Throw away old makeup so you don't waste time sorting through the old to find current colors.)

Problem: The computer seems to be consuming more and more of my time. Turn off the e-mail notification so you won't be tempted by the "You have mail" chime when you're in the middle of something else. Do you really need the information you're surfing the web for? Keep a kitchen timer by your computer to help you keep track of how long you've spent online. The same goes for chatting with friends. Limit Internet chat time the same way you limit phone time.

Problem: I always seem to run out of panty hose on workday mornings, necessitating a run to the store on the way to work. Buy panty hose in bulk three or four times a year when they're on sale. Keep hose with holes—the ones you can wear under pants—in a separate place from your regular ones.

Problem: We end up spending too much and too irresponsibly on birthday gifts because we wait until the last minute. Keep a few generic gifts on hand (picture frames, candles, books). Gift certificates to toy or sports stores and theaters are also good choices.

Problem: We often find ourselves in driving dilemmas because the kids have so many activities. Arrange all necessary transportation as early as possible—at least a day in advance. Hire a responsible teenager to help with errands and car pools. (You may need to evaluate your children's schedules. It may be that they are enrolled in too many extracurricular activities.)

Problem: Running simple errands seems to take twice as long as it should. I always have to go back to stores because I forgot something. Before you run errands, write down everywhere you need to go and plan the most expeditious route. Also, try to run errands at times of day when others don't.

Problem: I'm often late to work because I can't decide what to wear. Decide the night before what you will wear and how best to accessorize. Have your kids do this, too. Be sure to check for missing buttons, spots, and sagging hemlines.

Problem: Whenever there are two of something—socks, shoes, gloves—one always winds up missing when the kids are running out to meet the school bus. Have kids pick up all belongings before bed. Then have them set out all clothing and gear for the next day. Also, create an "Orphan Box" for socks, shoes, and gloves that are missing their mates. When the missing items reappear, you can easily find their match and put them away.

Problem: I spend too time searching for gift wrap, bows, and tape when I'm preparing a present. Set up a wrapping station in a large drawer or portable plastic crate and keep it stocked with various kinds of wrapping paper, ribbon, tape, scissors, gift bags, and tags.

Problem: Numerous trips to the post office, bank, and grocery store take up my whole lunch hour. Set up a mailing center in your home. Include a small postal scale, various denominations of stamps, different sizes of envelopes and padded mailers, boxes, and a postal rate chart. Then you can drop off packages on your way to work or mail right from home.

Set up automatic payroll deposit through your employer. Or have a set time once a week when you go to the bank. (Avoid Fridays.)

Plan menus during the weekend for the coming week. Shop once a week at a less-crowded time (late at night or early in the morning).

Problem: I get so frustrated when I'm put on hold for long periods. If you can't hold, say so. Otherwise, while waiting, multitask and get something else done: Balance your checkbook, clean out your purse, declutter a drawer, dust a shelf.

Problem: Heavy traffic affects my blood pressure. Avoid running errands during the lunch hour or 5 o'clock rush. Shopping right when stores open or right before they close is usually faster. Shop on the Internet whenever possible.

Problem: I tend to put big projects off . . . and off . . . and off. Decide to do something (even if it's something small) every day toward accomplishing projects you've let pile up.

Problem: When going to a new place, I spend a lot of time driving in circles because I don't have good directions or a map. Keep a map in the glove compartment of your car. Before you leave, write down the address and phone number of the places you're going. Visit www.mapquest.com and print off directions to your destination.

Problem: I'm always writing down the same things: baby-sitter instructions, grocery lists, medical emergency releases, travel lists, and so on. Use forms for all these things. (These forms are available at www.familymanager.com. If you don't have a computer and printer, handwrite the forms and have them duplicated at a printing center.)

Problem: Our family always runs out of essentials like toilet paper. Make a list of what supplies—cleaning products, toiletries, personal hygiene, paper products— you need at the first of every month and then buy them. Have a family rule that when someone uses up a product, he or she writes it down on the supply list.

Problem: I spend too much time cleaning up my kids' toy pieces. Keep a clean dustpan in your child's room to scoop up toys.

Problem: I waste time searching for things I use often. Check to see if you're taking up prime storage space with any items you don't use frequently. Replace with more often-used ones.

Problem: It seems like a waste to repack the same toiletry items every time I travel. Purchase travel-size items/bottles for all your toiletries and keep them in your overnight bag.

Problem: TV time is draining away important homework and chore time. Limit television viewing to programs that are really worth your time. Accomplish something productive while watching television—fold laundry, exercise, dust furniture, polish shoes, brush the dog or cat.

PERSONAL MANAGEMENT

Problem: I don't have time to read the self-help books I'm interested in. Listen to inspiring audio books when you're waiting in the car pool line.

Problem: Discouragement is a daily struggle for me. Take time daily to read a chapter in a book that lifts your spirits. Make it a habit to spend five minutes a day listing the things you're doing right.

Problem: I forget to take my vitamins. Take your vitamins at the same time every day. Keep them easily accessible.

Problem: Exercise is always the first thing I scratch off my list when I get busy. Enroll in an exercise class you can attend at a certain time three times each week. If it's near your home of office, you'll be more likely to go.

Problem: I never seem to get up early enough. Figure out how much time you need in the morning for each task, then work backward from when you need to leave the house to set your wake-up time. Be sure to add ten to fifteen minutes extra to account for the unexpected.

Problem: I have so much to do, I don't know where to start. Know your priorities and use a Daily Hit List (see page 12) to order your day. Always ask, *Is there a better way to get this done? Can this job be delegated to someone else?* Try to do only what you can do.

Problem: I keep losing track of articles I wanted to read or recipes I wanted to clip out of magazines. When you read an article or recipe in a magazine or newspaper that you want to keep, tear it out and stick it in a large envelope until you have time to file it in the appropriate place.

Problem: Snacking is adding on the pounds. Be alert for times that you eat because you're nervous, not because you're hungry. Drink a big glass of water instead. And don't eat standing up; remember, cows graze.

Problem: I feel like a failure. I never have enough time to get everything done, and I make so many mistakes that I really feel useless. Beating up on yourself is counterproductive. Remember that everyone makes mistakes. Learn from what you did, and move on. Every morning is a chance to start over and make changes in how you're living.

Now's a Good Time to . . .

It's an old but true adage: Timing is everything. Keep up with home and family tasks by creating some monthly routines. Here's a list to guide you.

January is a good month to . . .

- Start a Santa fund. At the end of each day, drop loose change from pockets and purses in a container. (On average, Americans carry $1.28 in change.) If you save that much all year long, you'll have $467.20—a nice head start on funding next year's holiday.

- Take your address book/calendar to a card store and purchase all your cards for the entire year: birthdays, anniversaries, etc. Write events you want to remember on your calendar. Make a note one week before the date to send a present or card. Be sure to buy some extras, too.

- Organize photos. Set up a card table in an out-of-the-way place and work on putting photos in albums a few minutes at a time.

- Start gathering information needed to file income taxes. If you don't already have one, set up a filing system so information for next year's return will be at your fingertips.

February is a good month to . . .

■ Start sorting through household items and clothing for a spring garage sale.

■ Make out three weeks' worth of your family's favorite dinner menus. Recycle these menus all during the year.

■ Set a goal to clean out all closets and drawers. Tackle one closet and two or three drawers a week until you're done.

■ Begin or beef up a daily exercise routine to get ready for swimsuit season.

March is a good month to . . .

■ Have a decluttering campaign, then pick one weekend to spring-clean as a family.

■ Start planning your family summer vacation and make necessary reservations.

■ Research summer activity options for your kids.

April is a good month to . . .

■ Clean out and organize your garage.

■ Have a garage sale. (Schedule it near the first or fifteenth of the month. That's when most people get paid and have more money to spend.)

■ Go through your makeup and discard what's old and dried out. Replace darker colors with lighter ones for spring.

May is a good month to . . .

■ Mothproof and store winter clothes.

■ Hire a chimney sweep to clean soot, remove birds' nests, and inspect for cracks.

■ Check on summer classes and programs offered through your local library, museum, YMCA, community colleges, or parks and recreation departments.

June is a good month to . . .

- Get ready for outdoor summer fun: Keep beach towels, kids' water-play toys, and sunscreen in an easy-access place.

- Reorganize your kitchen and storage areas a bit for impromptu picnics and summer suppers outside.

- Plan a family outing each week and write it on your calendar: Camp out at a nearby state or national park, go on a hike, or ride bikes.

July is a good month to . . .

- Buy fresh produce in bulk at a farmer's market to freeze or can.

- Buy a Christmas ornament when you're on vacation to save the memory.

- Have kids clean out their toys and sports equipment and go through drawers and closets to cull outgrown clothing and shoes.

- Shop sales for summer clothes and bathing suits.

August is a good month to . . .

- Shop for items that need to be replaced for school.

- Schedule a family meeting to discuss schedules and responsibilities for the upcoming school year.

- Set up a study area and store school supplies nearby in drawers or bins or on shelves.

- Have a "Good-Bye, Summer" party. Go to a theme park, a lake, or the beach for one last summer fling.

September is a good month to . . .

- Make a master list of things family members can do to help around the house when they have an extra five, fifteen, or thirty minutes.

- Begin updating names and addresses on your holiday greeting card list. Take a holiday-greeting-card family photograph.

- Make travel arrangements for the Thanksgiving holiday.

October is a good month to . . .

- Stock up on cold and flu medications. Check expiration dates of last year's medicines, and discard outdated items.

- Get a flu shot.

- Get out winter clothes, and store summer clothes.

- Make travel arrangements for the Christmas holidays.

- Have your car serviced for winter driving.

November is a good month to . . .

- Schedule first-of-the-new-year appointments for family members with physicians, dentists, optometrists, etc.

- Clean out your pantry. Throw out any expired items, and check for weevils in boxes and bags. Donate some items that are still good to a food bank or community service organization.

- Plan a holiday party.

December is a good month to . . .

- Work on your goals for the coming year.

- Reconnect with extended family and old friends.

- Give yourself the freedom to enjoy the holidays.

- Show your appreciation to people who help and serve you throughout the year.

Working from Home

Working from home, either independently or telecommuting, is becoming more popular and doable for many dual-career women. Here are six questions to help you decide if it's a viable alternative for you:

1. Are you self-directed, and do you work well independently? In past evaluations, how has your employer rated you on time management and productivity? If you received good scores, it's positive evidence you can use to prove to your employer (or yourself) that you can work at home.

2. Realistically, can your job be done away from a corporate office environment? Does it require uninterrupted concentration? Do you need a lot of space and special equipment? Can your job be done using a computer, fax, modem, e-mail, pager, and/or voicemail? Will the company provide those? If not, can you cover the costs?

3. Would a compressed workweek—three twelve-hour days or four ten-hour days—work as well or better than your current system?

4. How will your boss supervise you? How often will you need to attend meetings at the office? Can he or she evaluate your work if you work at home?

5. What benefits can you sell to your employer? Less days off work (a sick child no longer means missed hours)? Increased flexibility to meet client and corporate needs—special projects can be done after regular work hours? Reduced need for office and parking? Increased employee satisfaction? The company will save money if you reduce your hours? The key to negotiating the job schedule you want is to make your employer see that he or she will gain from the arrangement as well.

6. If you lose some or all of your benefits, can you afford to cover them yourself?

If telecommuting/working from home looks viable for you after answering these questions, research child-care options. Find short-term child care for your children when you are away from home. Also, have a child-care plan during the summer. Be sure your employer knows that you will not care for your children on company time.

Then write a formal proposal that states your request to work from home. Include the date you want to start. Summarize why you believe your job is appropriate for telecommuting, and describe your proposed daily routine. Suggest a specified length of time for a trial period. Remember that your boss might need approval from another management level, especially if your company has never had an employee work from home. A well-written proposal will get him or her on your side.

Home Office Sanity Savers

One of the biggest pluses of telecommuting or working in a home-based business is the flexibility. But being able to balance your paying job with your Family Manager job requires an extra dose of discipline and organization, as well as setting some basic house rules with your family.

Here are some guidelines on how to achieve that balance:

- If you've got young kids at home, hire someone to watch your children while you work. This will allow you to work for several, focused hours at a clip rather than having to wait for naps or evening. Consider trading child care with other mothers from preschool or your neighborhood.

- If you choose not to hire a sitter, you must be extremely disciplined with your time. Work your schedule around your child's nap or preschool hours, and create a backup plan for days when your child won't nap, has vacation, or is home sick from preschool.

- Screen all phone calls with an answering machine or voicemail while your child is in preschool, school, or day care to protect your high-focus time.

- Develop phone rules. One mom painted a Ping-Pong paddle red on one side and green on the other. When she's on a casual personal call, she holds up the green side, and when the children need to be silent and wait (barring an emergency), she holds up the red side. Reward your children for following the rules.

> Open accounts with companies that furnish at-home delivery and pick-up.

- Establish workspace boundaries. Being able to work behind a closed door is ideal for eliminating distractions. If that's impossible, have some sort of indicators that mark out your work zone; for example, those orange cones you can buy at sports equipment stores. You need something that alerts passersby that "Mommy is working—do not disturb."

- Think of projects in their component parts. If you don't have time to finish a whole thing, use the time to finish parts of it.

- Set up a "home office" for your child with art supplies, paper, pencils, tape, and an old briefcase. When my son was a toddler, one of his favorite games became "working," and he became so engrossed in it that I got extra chunks of time to work.

- Schedule specific personal time for chores, errands, exercise, time with friends, and so on. The flexibility of blending home and other work make it tempting to whittle away your productivity with housework, errands, or just chatting on the phone with friends.

Passing Time in Meaningful Ways

Did you know that the average American spends twenty-seven hours each year sitting at traffic lights? Whether you're waiting at a red light, in the doctor's office, in a car pool line, or at a restaurant, this time doesn't have to be wasted. The secret to effective time management is using small bits of time well. But the idea is not to just do more. It's to create time to do more that matters.

While you're waiting . . .

BUILD RELATIONSHIPS.
- Use drive time to broach a difficult subject with your child. Sometimes it's less threatening to discuss a sensitive matter when you're both staring out a

"Do what you can, with what you have, where you are."
—Theodore Roosevelt

windshield. Turn down the radio and make comments that affirm your child, such as an improvement you see in a particular area. Ask how you can help him or her move toward a goal or succeed at an undertaking. As you affirm him or her, add a light touch of your hand to your words.

- Use long drives to talk to your husband about important matters such as goals and priorities for your family. Ask him about his world—what he enjoys most, what's difficult for him, how you can support him, etc.

- While you're waiting for your food to be served at a restaurant, have everyone in the family dream aloud about what they'd like to see happening in their lives five years from now.

- If you're early to an appointment, write a note or call a friend you need to catch up with.

LEARN SOMETHING NEW.
- Listen to an audiobook while you're stuck in traffic.

- Keep a small dictionary and a crossword puzzle handy. Stretch your mental muscles.

- Keep a magazine or book in your purse to read while you wait.

- Ask questions—find out how something is made, how something works, or why something is done a particular way.

- Ask your child to explain something he or she is learning in school. You'll make your child feel like a genius and refresh your own mind in the process.

- Ask someone about their job—what they like most and least about it.

- Listen to talk radio and contemplate the news or issues.

DREAM.
- Consider the future for your children—their abilities, their character, their accomplishments, etc. What could you do today to help them toward success?

■ Imagine yourself as successful in a particular pursuit—a tennis tournament, a weight-loss effort, a project at work, or starting a business. Let the good feeling motivate you to keep working toward success.

■ Plan your grocery list, your next clothing purchase, your next vacation, a party, how to confront a friend about a problem, or a romantic rendezvous with your husband.

ENCOURAGE SOMEONE.

■ Call someone who lost a loved one in the last year, and let him or her know you are still thinking of them.

■ Write to your mom or dad.

■ Write a congratulations note to someone who got a promotion or was successful on a project or event.

■ Say something pleasant to someone around you, and experience the pleasure of adding to the enjoyment of someone else's day.

Save Your
Children's Day

Motherhood is serious business. It is not only a great privilege to raise children, but also a profession we need to take as seriously as anything else we deem important in life. In a nutshell, the job takes courage, consistency, and commitment—whether it's discovering and working with how our children are designed, knowing when and how to discipline, teaching siblings how to get along, understanding how teenagers operate, passing on our values, or making memories as a family—because we moms wield a lot of power.

In this section, you will learn commonsense, easy-to-apply strategies I've collected and tested over the past thirty years of motherhood. There are ideas for fostering loving, lasting relationships and helping our children connect in meaningful ways with each other, with the outside world, and perhaps most important, with their own talents, skills, and spirits.

> * "By wisdom a house is built, and through understanding it is established; through knowledge its rooms are filled with rare and beautiful treasures."
> —The Book of Proverbs

You'll also find advice on how to create an environment in your home where children and parents alike can experience a more peaceful, positive life. Some of the ideas are results of my victories; some I've learned through defeat. Use them to stimulate your own thoughts, plans, and dreams for your children. Start by setting some simple goals and acting on a few ideas that seem like a comfortable fit for your family scenario and operating style. Keep in mind that small changes can make a huge difference.

Above all else, please underscore this in your mind: All your learning, patience, hard work, and unconditional love *will* pay off. I promise. Today my family is my greatest joy. We are committed to each other's best interests. We feed each other's souls, and we enjoy each other's company. I truly believe that the development and nurturing of human beings is a Family Manager's most vital mission. In our home, and through our teaching and example, our children learn who they are and how to be that way, and ultimately how to succeed in life.

Seven Ways to Be a Great Mom

Anyone can be a great mom. It's true! It doesn't take a Ph.D. in child development or a big bank account to raise children who feel loved, listened to, and supported. All it takes is adherence to a few basic principles to guide you in every situation—no matter how many kids you have or how different they are.

When our first child was born, we wanted to give him the best of everything, which was hard because we were on the starve-as-you-go plan in graduate school. Now, thirty years and two more children later, I am glad we have not ever been able to give our kids "the best of everything"—at least in the way I thought about it at first.

Don't get me wrong. It's a good thing to provide our children with the toys, tools, and tutors that will enhance their development. But there are other "gifts," if you will, that are far more important. No matter what your bank account, being a great mother will be more valuable than anything else you'll ever give your kids. Here are seven things every mom can do:

1. Be Available

Children need to know we are there for them when they need us to be. This doesn't mean you schedule your life according to your child's whims. It is not healthy for a child to think the universe revolves around him or her. Availability means you are open, and you give yourself willingly, without regret. If you have a busy schedule, make it a priority to carve out time to give each child focused attention.

The mother of two elementary-age children recently asked for my opinion about a dilemma she was facing. The company where she worked was restructuring, and she was given two options: take another position, which would mean longer hours but higher pay, or go part-time at her present position and take a sizeable pay cut.

> "Could I turn back the time machine, I would double the attention I gave my children and go to fewer meetings."
> —J. D. Eppings

I empathized, as I had once faced a similar decision. When I had children, my husband and I decided it was important for me to be home as much as possible. So while I worked at part-time jobs here and there, my college friends were climbing the corporate ladder. I confess there were days when I envied them the new furniture, fancy cars, and nice vacations they could afford. But thirty years later, I can say with passion and confidence, the choice paid off—and is still paying off—in inestimable ways.

Every family is different, and every mom and dad must do what works best for their family. In the families of two good friends, the fathers scaled back their careers to be home with the kids while the mothers work full-time. This setup works very well for them.

If you're facing the "How much should I work outside the home?" dilemma, keep these two principles in mind: First, someone is going to raise your kids and teach them values. Do everything you can to ensure that they are *your* values. Second, if you have the choice between raising your kids on expensive carpet or linoleum, go for the linoleum—if it means being able to spend more time with your children.

2. Be Lavish with Love and Forgiveness

Assure your children that they are loved and accepted even when they fail. Never withhold physical or eye contact, even when they make mistakes or disappoint you. Be sure they know that although you disapprove of their attitude or actions, your love is unconditional. Hug, hold, and touch your child in appropriate, loving ways every day. Look into their eyes regularly and tell them how much you love them.

> "Children need love, especially when they do not deserve it."
> —Harold S. Hulbert

Twenty-five Things You Should Never Say to a Child

1. You're just no good.
2. You'll never amount to anything.
3. You got what you deserved.
4. What's wrong with you?
5. When are you going to act your age?
6. Can't you do anything right?
7. I've had it with you.
8. All you ever do is cause trouble.
9. Just wait until you have kids.
10. When will you ever learn?
11. You are stupid.
12. You are lazy.
13. Who do you think you are?
14. You'll be the death of me yet.
15. Haven't I taught you anything?
16. You need to have your head examined.
17. Don't you care about anything?
18. What makes you think you're so special?
19. Don't you ever listen?
20. When are you going to start obeying me?
21. If I've told you once, I've told you a million times.
22. I can't wait until you're gone.
23. Why can't you be more like your sister?
24. You are so much trouble.
25. I don't know why I had kids.

3. Be Generous with Praise

Children never grow out of needing heavy doses of praise—no matter what their ages. The five-to-one praise principle is a good rule of thumb to follow: Balance every negative comment you make to a child with five positive comments. Think before you speak. Ask yourself if what you want to say will build up or tear down your child. Each day, look for ways to affirm your child's unique giftedness and personality. Encourage others in the family to do the same with each other.

There are times in every child's life when it's hard to maintain the five-to-one ratio. But it's important that we keep looking for the positives. They're there.

And keep in mind that praise and encouragement mean different things to different people. We must understand how each of our children likes to be applauded or praised, because each might have a different preference. One child might feel very special when you praise him privately, one-on-one. Another child might appreciate praise in front of other people. Still another might long for something tangible, such as a small gift, or a card or letter with a sincere message of praise.

> "A torn jacket is soon mended, but hard words bruise the heart of a child."
>
> —Henry Wadsworth Longfellow

Twenty-five Things You Can't Say Enough to a Child.

1. It is such a blessing to be your mom.
2. You're an incredible person.
3. You did that so well.
4. If more kids were like you, the world would be a better place.
5. It's so good to be with you.
6. You're the best!
7. You are such a nice person.
8. You're learning fast.
9. You mean so much to me.
10. You are very bright.
11. You have unlimited potential.
12. You're on the right track now.
13. You're getting the hang of it.
14. That's the best you've ever done.
15. You're getting better every day.
16. You're such a quick learner.
17. I appreciate your attitude.
18. I can tell you are trying.
19. I knew you could do it.
20. Keep up the good work.
21. You are a real trooper.
22. You did a great job.
23. I believe in you.
24. You're going to go far in life.
25. If someone lined up all the four-year-olds (use your child's age) in the world and told me I could pick any one I wanted, I'd choose you.

4. Be Fair

We all ascribe to the fact that people are different—in theory. But when we have to live with the peculiarities of the people in our home, the standard operating procedure seems to be "fix and repair" rather than "accept and affirm." There will be things about our children that annoy us, and there will be times they blatantly disobey. But before we get out the tool kit, we should stop and ask, *Is this my child's problem or mine? Is there really a "perfect" way to take out the garbage, clean a room, or get homework done? Is there something inherently wrong with what my child is doing, or is she just not doing it my way?*

To be fair with our children, it's extremely important to discover *why* they misbehave, don't cooperate, or ignore our leadership. There are several reasons why children disobey and violate our expectations. Each reason demands an appropriate, fair response.

- **They don't understand.** Sometimes a child simply does not know he or she did something wrong. This can stem from either our failure to communicate or

"The applause of a single human being is of great consequence."
—Samuel Johnson

the child's inability to comprehend. If this is case, the child needs clarification of the issue—not punishment. Especially with a young child, a fair response to disobedience is to ask, "Did you understand you were not supposed to . . . ?"

■ **They didn't remember.** Sometimes children forget because they don't take us seriously, but we need to recognize and respond fairly to honest memory lapses. This is a constant problem with younger children. Sometimes it helps to give a child a reminder and a warning concerning the consequences of regular forgetfulness: If she forgets to take her lunch to school, she'll have to deal with it. Some kids, because of special learning styles, have difficulty remembering a series of instructions. Rather than telling them what you want them to do, you might write down or demonstrate it. Some children retain/learn information better this way.

■ **They are not capable.** Sometimes children are physically, mentally, or emotionally incapable of following the rules. A chronic problem in many parents is having unrealistic expectations of younger children. Milk will be spilled, not because a five-year-old is being careless, but because his hands are small and uncoordinated. Before reacting harshly to apparent misbehavior, stop and ask yourself if your expectations are appropriate to the child's capability to respond. It's not fair to ask children to behave beyond their years.

■ **They don't trust us.** A vast difference can exist between a child's perspective and a parent's perspective of a problem. For example, I'll never forget the day I was getting madder by the minute because I thought our oldest son was just being stubborn about a little splinter in his finger. When my husband and I sat him up on the bathroom counter, holding both of his legs and hands, and said, "Sit still. This won't hurt," his crying escalated to screaming and his wiggling to writhing. Then we realized that having a splinter removed with a needle was as traumatic to a young child as major surgery without anesthesia would be to either of us. He didn't know that he would feel better once the splinter was out. Our son had no basis from which to trust us, because, instead of listening to his fears, we told him he was making a mountain out of a molehill. Sometimes molehills are mountains from a child's perspective.

■ **They simply want their own way.** Much misbehavior and failure to comply comes down to a battle of the wills. When a child thinks, *I'm going to do what I want to do when I want to do it*—whether the child is six or sixteen—fair and appropriate discipline is the only answer.

5. Be Firm

Discipline is much more than the ability to send a child to a corner for a time-out, skillfully wield a wooden spoon, or take away the car keys. The goal of all discipline is to change the way a child thinks so he can, in turn, change his own behavior and become a self-disciplined person.

Raising children requires a savvy understanding of the unique forms of discipline and when each is the most effective method you can use to call forth strong character and choices. You will use each of these at different times in your child's life:

■ Instructive discipline—explaining the acts and attitudes that we, the parents, have decided are not acceptable.

■ Modeling discipline—exhibiting the behavior we want our children to practice.

■ Corrective discipline—rebuking bad behavior to call on the child's character to change.

■ Reward discipline—praising a child for things he or she does right.

■ Punishment discipline—denying privileges to demonstrate the consequences of unwise choices.

Standing Firm with Older Kids

Countless mothers tell me they are exasperated because their kids won't obey or cooperate. If your child is one of them, consider the following questions: Does your son or daughter talk on the phone? Does he or she watch TV? Play video or computer games? Does he or she like to borrow the car and go out with friends?

Those activities, and others like them, are *privileges*, not rights. We do our kids a favor when we have a policy that says, "Unless you obey and cooperate, you do not get your privileges. Period." Granted, kids won't like this—but they'll bow to it. Properly motivated, kids will do anything.

Even more important than the child's cooperation is the lesson he or she learns about real life. After all, that's the way the adult world operates. If you don't obey the chain of command on your job, you won't have the privilege of getting a paycheck or maybe even having a job at all.

Don't be afraid to trade permission for obedience. Your child deserves to learn this at home, where the stakes are small, rather than in the cold, cruel world, where the stakes are enormous.

Laughter Is Good Medicine

Laughter is an inestimable blessing of life, and it is something children come prewired to do. Studies have shown that human beings laugh more when they are four years old than at any other time in life, but from that time forward, the number of times we laugh each day decreases. This is more serious than it might sound. Laugher causes our brain to create endorphins that relieve stress and activate the immune system.

Help your child cultivate this innate trait. Laugh at yourself and with others. Teach your child to do the same. Make it a high priority as a family to laugh and have fun together.

6. Be Fun

Strange as it seems, having fun with your children has a great deal to do with how they respond to your firmness. The moments you spend laughing, playing, and enjoying life together make large deposits in your children's emotional bank account. They understand your love and commitment to them in tangible ways. So when the time comes for you to be firm and administer discipline, their accounts are sufficient to stand a withdrawal.

I've met a lot of parents who allow overly busy schedules and the stresses of life to crowd out taking time to have fun. The results are not pretty: They begin to take life, and themselves, too seriously. They feel guilty for not playing with and relishing their family, so they rationalize their feelings by saying they choose "quality time" over quantity of time. They tuck in moments with their children between meetings, appointments, or other "important work." The problem is that we can't fool our kids into thinking we're enjoying spending time with them when our minds are someplace else.

Other parents are physically with their children for longer periods of time but are not really *with* them. Sitting in front of the television together or working in front of a computer screen with the child in a nearby room isn't making a substantive emotional investment. When it comes to parenting, I believe quality time and quantity time are like the oxygen we breathe. The quantity determines whether we live or die, but the quality of the oxygen determines how well we live.

7. Be Humble

Because our children don't come with handling instructions, every parent will make mistakes. As you try to customize your parenting for each child, try to remember that your children don't need an expert, they need a guide. When you blow it, just admit it, learn from it, then get up and go on. Far from undermining your position, this humility will say to the child in the most powerful way, "I am really for you. I am not trying to make you something you are not. I love you, and I am on your team."

House Rules

When parents ask me what's one thing they can do to get their family and the atmosphere in their home back on track, I tell them to start here. House rules are important tools for peaceful family living that benefit the whole family. Everyone knows what to expect and what is expected of him. We wrote ours early in our family history, and they've evolved over the years to apply to the ages of our children.

Creating your own set of house rules to help you maintain some semblance of order can save a lot of emotional energy that would have been used to fuss and argue. But there are long-term benefits also. The relational skills your kids learn at home—respecting others' feelings and their property—will make it easier for them to form healthy relationships with friends, college roommates, their spouses, co-workers, and associates in the future.

> * "I always wondered about where 'kingdom come' might be, since my mother threatened so many times to knock me there."
> —Bill Cosby

If you decide to write your own house rules (which I highly recommend), you can use ours as a model. Our rules are not perfect, and they keep changing—which is an important point for all of us to remember: Stay flexible. Kids grow, situations change, and schedules get altered.

Peel Team Big Ten House Rules

Rule 1: **We're all in this together.** The rules apply to everyone—Mom and Dad, too. Kids won't buy a double standard. When you give them permission to call you on a violation, they will feel ownership of the rules. Albert Schweitzer was right when he said, "Example isn't the most important thing, example is the only thing." We must practice what we preach.

A woman told me that her children were behaving rudely toward each other and asked for my advice. In the course of the conversation, I learned that she and her husband were in the habit of making sarcastic, disrespectful remarks to each other. We talked about the importance of being good role models for our children. She answered her own question, then went home and asked her husband if they could agree to stop their own childish behavior. In a family meeting, they confessed their less-than-optimum example to the kids. She reported back to me that the atmosphere in their home had changed remarkably for the better.

> "It is not fair to ask of others what you are not willing to do yourself." —Eleanor Roosevelt

Let kids who are old enough have a say in how rules you agree to abide by as a family work both ways. For example, when you talk about housekeeping guidelines, a child's rule might be, "Don't leave wet towels on the bathroom floor." One of Mom's rules might be, "Don't go ballistic when someone leaves a wet towel on the bathroom floor."

Rule 2. **No yelling at anyone or "pitching fits."** In our home, we reserve yelling and screaming for emergencies only. Authority does not increase with volume. Lay down the rule about yelling and enforce the consequences. "Outside voices" are not to be used inside, and yelling at others is not tolerated. And remember, the moment you are drawn into a yelling match, you surrender parental authority to the strength of the personalities involved. When you are tempted to raise your voice in a show of authority, try to think of something Margaret Thatcher said: "Being powerful is like being a lady. If you have to tell people you are, you aren't." If I have to raise my voice to prove I'm in authority, then I'm not.

When we are emotionally wound up, our voices magnify. Be aware of this when dealing with a problem. Slow down your speech. This will help you speak in a more gentle tone of voice.

If you're really riled and aren't sure you can control your feelings, get away for a few minutes to regroup. If you can't get away, force yourself to count to 100 slowly. Once *you've* calmed down, you can lay down the law with your kids about talking things over calmly.

"No pitching fits" was an early rule with consequences when our boys were small. From an early age, children need to know this is not acceptable behavior. We had a parental guideline: We never gave the desired response when a child used pitching a fit as a means of getting it. As children are able to understand, explain the consequences and follow through. Teach your kids alternative ways to ask for what they want or express in a controlled way how they feel.

Teaching Kids What to Do with Anger

Part of being human is getting angry, sometimes for good reason. But teaching our children how to express anger in healthy ways, as well as how to deal with their own faults—to ask for and receive forgiveness from themselves and others— is perhaps one of the biggest gifts we can give them.

Living in a family means learning to put the feelings of others before our own. Our responsibility is to teach and show by example what to do with uncomfortable feelings such as anger. This means that Mom and Dad exhibit self-control even though they feel like slamming a door, throwing something breakable, or hitting someone.

Here are some tips for teaching children how to manage this powerful emotion.

■ Decide in your family how you will and will not express anger. For example: Never go to bed angry at each other. Settle disputes as soon as possible. We do not hit each other, no matter what. (Let your kids help in setting the guidelines.)

■ Create a safe place to discuss past offenses family members are still angry about. Set aside regular times for family meetings to discern ongoing problems so resentments won't build up. Sit down and talk about these honestly. Make sure everyone has an opportunity to add to the agenda.

■ If expressing anger physically is typical in your family, remember that a home that condones violence is the breeding ground for loneliness and depression in children. Seek counsel from a pastor or family therapist if you need help.

■ Be aware that viewing violence on TV and in movies increases aggressiveness, instills fear of becoming a victim, promotes indifference to victims of violence, and stimulates the appetite for more violence. Decide what you will allow your children to watch, and stick to your decision. Oversee their TV viewing by making sure they turn on the TV to see a specific show, not just to see what's on.

■ Physical exercise is a good way to relieve angry feelings. Send yourself or your angry children to walk around the block a few times.

■ All of us lose our tempers at times. When this happens, ask forgiveness and move on. Don't wallow in guilt. Don't abdicate your responsibility just because you make mistakes periodically. Ask forgiveness, and give it.

■ Identify the consistent conflicts in your home that cause tempers to flair: who didn't do what they said they would do, how many minutes someone gets to play a video game, how much time is spent on the computer or telephone, etc. Add specific issues to your house rules that map out simple guidelines of fairness.

■ Coach your child's baseball, soccer, or other sports team. This is a great opportunity to teach that good losers are winners, and bad winners are losers.

■ Remember there are always two sides to every issue. When you're called upon to referee an argument between your children, be sure to get all the facts.

■ Let your children see you deal with anger and frustration in a positive way. It is unreasonable to expect your children to heed your advice and ignore your example.

Rule 3: **Delete the phrase "Shut up!" from our vocabulary entirely.** Every human being is a worthwhile, uniquely made individual, worthy of respect. Don't tolerate these or any other disrespectful or devaluing words between family members. Be sure everyone knows offenders will face consequences.

> "There are two sides to every question." —**Protagoras**

We taught our children that when a sibling got on their nerves or interrupted a conversation, they were allowed to say, "Please be quiet." Because kids will be kids and sometimes don't want to comply with the requests of a sibling, if the offender did not voluntarily refrain from "bugging" or talking by the third request, a judge (usually a parent) was brought in and we sat down and talked about what was going on. Many times the behavior was just to annoy the brother who was asking for silence. In that case, I dealt with the annoying behavior and talked to the offender about the importance of showing preference to others above ourselves.

Rule 4: **Calling names, or making unkind, cutting remarks to each other is strictly out of order.** There's an old saying: "To belittle is to be little." Talk to your children about the meaning of this saying. Help them understand that they're being small persons if they find it necessary to cut someone else down.

The fact that we laugh a lot with and at each other is one of the things I enjoy most about our family. But every family must have boundaries. Some comments are definitely out of bounds and do not fall into the category of playful teasing. It's important that when family members poke fun at one another, it's fun for everyone. It's not funny to joke about someone's big nose, deformities, seemingly stupid mistakes, fears, or weaknesses. If a comment made in a joking manner hurts feelings, be sure to talk it out so it won't happen again.

Make a list of the names and negative phrases you would like to eliminate from your family's vocabulary: "Shut up," "Dummy," "Stupid," "Punk," "I don't like you," "You make me sick." Talk about how each person feels when these things are said to him. Set a family goal to rid these terms and phrases from your conversation. Put each person in charge of him- or herself. Create a chart with each person's name. Put a check mark by the name of the person who has a slip of the tongue and uses one of the off-limit words or phrases.

Rule 5: **Take responsibility for our own actions and words.** Children need help learning how to work through conflicts. They don't know how to do this instinctively. When your kids get into a fight, sit them down and hear both sides of the story. Ask questions that make each one think about both sides of the problem. Guide them to discover what the root problem really is and focus on their behavior—not what was done to them.

Help your children learn the principle that small people blame others for their mistakes and actions. Make them aware of the fact that they are always responsible for their own actions and that you hold them responsible for their actions—no matter what the other person does. There is no excuse for poor behavior, a poor response, or blaming someone else for our problem.

The Swine Fine Bucket

When our kids were old enough to have money of their own, I created Swine Fine bucket. I painted a picture of a pig on the top of a white plastic bucket and kept it on the kitchen counter. Whenever one of the boys behaved disrespectfully toward a family member or exhibited poor manners, I called out "Swine fine!" They were required to deposit a designated amount of money (which I got to keep) in my bucket.

Rule 6: **Ask forgiveness when they have hurt or offended someone, even if it was an accident.** Sometimes it's hard for kids to see the importance of restoring a relationship—especially if they can't see they did anything wrong. It's important that we teach them to try to feel the other person's pain or discomfort. Be sure you set the example by apologizing when you hurt or disappoint them—even if it was unintentional. Saying "I'm sorry" or "I was wrong" won't undermine your authority. Living a double standard will.

Rule 7: **Keep confidential what we share with each other.** Your children need to know they can trust you. Create a safe environment for communication. Here's an important question: When your son or daughter comes face-to-face with a temptation or difficult situation and is struggling with what to do, will he or she want to talk to you? Are you considered a safe, supportive, and reliable source of counsel they can trust?

Don't talk about one child's problems to another child. And don't talk to your friends about confidential matters your child shares with you. I know a mother who damaged her own daughter's reputation and their relationship by openly talking to other mothers about how she couldn't trust her daughter. Although the daughter had abused her mother's trust only once by sneaking out with an older boy before she was permitted to date, when the news traveled, those who heard the rumor blew the occurrence way out of proportion. The mother and the daughter became estranged.

In another instance, a mother learned her teenage son had been drinking. They openly talked about this and dealt with his behavior firmly, but lovingly, in the privacy of their family. Although he made some bad choices, today this boy has a shining reputation and a wonderful relationship with his parents.

Rule 8: **Respect each other's space.** Everyone needs a degree of privacy. We made a habit of always knocking before opening someone's closed door. All children need to have a sense of ownership and privacy. They need a place where they can daydream, try on clothes, experiment with makeup, practice shaving, and lie down quietly after a demanding day at school. Talk openly about giving one another space and respecting others' feelings.

When our oldest boys were teenagers, they shared a room. They had to learn to give each other privacy when needed. And because one of the boys could tolerate more mess than his orderly brother, they had to learn to think of each other's feelings and cut each other slack in this area as well.

When a family lives together in restricted space, it's important for everyone to be aware that sound travels, and what a person does in one room affects others in a room nearby. This means when the boys turned on music in their room, they needed to recognize that I was down the hall, trying to finish a magazine article. It also meant that when my husband or I considered turning on the TV on a school night, we thought twice about it if a boy had not finished his homework or was trying to study for a test.

Rule 9: **Respect each other's stuff.** I am amazed at the way some children mistreat the property of others. We've had guests break toys, appliances, and furniture—without even so much as an "I'm sorry" from the child or the parents. One afternoon a neighborhood child broke a brand-new, twenty-dollar toy James had saved his money for and bought that morning. Without even a word of apology, the child just left and didn't come back for two weeks.

We all want our children to learn to respect the property of others and share their belongings with others. To do this, they must have a sense of control over their things and respect the control someone else has over his or her things. This meant if James had a friend over and they wanted to play with something that belonged to a big brother who wasn't home to give his permission, then they had to find something else to play with. It meant if Joel wanted to wear a sweater of John's, he had to ask John first. It also means I respect their property as well.

Years ago, we moved into a new house. I enjoyed the process of decorating and creating an attractive, welcoming environment. I tackled our teenagers' room one day when they were at school. When they returned home, they gasped when I threatened to take their cola-can sculpture out of their window. "Mom, this is creative!" Creative, yes. Attractive, no. But in a rare moment of strength, I realized that it's important for them to create the teenager-friendly environment they'll enjoy than for me to win the House Beautiful award. And redoing their things without their approval would have been a violation of their privacy. We compromised: They kept the "sculpture" in the window but also agreed to keep the window shade pulled down behind it. As you can probably guess, their cola-can window treatment was never featured in a decorator magazine.

Rule 10: **Agree to abide by the family chore system and get together regularly for family team meetings.** Everyone who lives under the roof of a house should help with the upkeep. Identify the consistent conflicts in your home: whose turn it is to feed the dog, do the dishes, or vacuum the family room. Then schedule a family meeting and come armed with a list of chores to be divied up among family members. Create a chore chart so you'll know who's supposed to do what when.

Preparing for a New Baby

Among continuous rounds of laundry, playdates, and baseball games, you've just learned you're expecting another baby. You might wonder, in the midst of all the plates you're spinning now, how you'll incorporate a new human being and all its needs into your life. Relax. Mothers throughout the centuries have done it—and without all the organization and safety products we have today. Let the ideas in this section assist you in preparing for and welcoming this new little person and helping your family adjust with joy and peace.

> "A new baby is like the beginning of all things—wonder, hope, a dream of possibilities."
> —Eda J. Le Shan

Getting Ready for Delivery Day

The day a baby arrives is a joyous one, and family members near and far love to herald the birth of a brand-new human being in their midst. Your parents, extended family, and friends will likely want to visit and "help." Although well intentioned, all these people can actually create more work than they help. At the same time, siblings are excited about their new brother or sister but might feel ignored in all the hoopla. Here are some tips for sharing the joy without getting a headache—and for smoothing the adjustment period for siblings:

> "There was never a child so lovely but his mother was glad to get asleep." —Ralph Waldo Emerson

BEFORE THE BIRTH:
- Be clear, in a gracious way, whether you and your husband want any family or friends in the waiting room, birthing or delivery room, or at home when

you return with the baby. Stick to your decision, no matter who tries to enforce his or her preferences on you.

■ Create a list of tasks people can do when they ask if they can help. This way you can take them up on their offers in practical ways once the baby is born. For those eager to help, in addition to bringing in meals, let them do laundry, run errands, and chauffer older kids to their various commitments. They could also baby-sit one night a week so you and your husband could go out.

AFTER THE BIRTH:

■ In the first few days at home, explain to young children that you need to rest. In age-appropriate ways, tell them that having a baby makes big changes in your body but that you'll soon be back to your old self.

■ Without guilt, take the personal time you need to bond with your child.

■ Avoid drop-ins when you or your baby are sleeping by hanging a friendly "Do not disturb—family napping" sign on the front door.

■ Take lots of pictures to share with relatives who can't be close.

■ Show some extra affection to the baby's siblings. A wonderful book to give the older brother or sister is either *I'm the Big Sister* or *I'm the Big*

Helping Kids Cope with Change

A new baby brother or sister can stir up all sorts of issues and fears for children. Use these ideas to smooth the transition.

1. Have a family meeting to announce the blessed event. Consider the ages of your children—a kindergartner might be able to handle news of a new baby sooner than a teenager would. If anyone raises objections to the change, don't get defensive—be honest about your own apprehensions.

2. Present the change in a positive light, even if you have mixed feelings yourself. Don't say, "I don't know how we can fit another person into our already crowded house and schedule." Do say, "It's going to be exciting to all work together to fit the baby into our family."

3. Talk about the change often. Bring it up in daily conversation. Start a countdown on the calendar. Be aware that acting out is often kids' way of expressing their insecurity—talk with them. Let them know how much you love them and what great big brothers or sisters they will be.

4. Consider giving each family member a notebook in which to record his or her feelings about the impending change. Young children can draw their ideas. (Be sure you and your spouse talk through your own feelings and present a united front to your kids.)

5. Spend private time with each child so he or she can share concerns and receive reassurance of your love.

Brother, both by Susan Russell Ligon (Tommy Nelson, 2002). Try to spend a few minutes alone with each child each day. Ask about each one's day, or read a favorite book together. Let them talk about their concerns.

■ Give siblings time to adjust. No matter how much you've prepared them, the reality takes time to sink in.

Childproofing Your Home

When you become a parent, whether you're a rookie or a seasoned player, you need to get down on your hands and knees (literally) and look at your home from the vantage point of a baby who is just learning to crawl and a curious toddler. According to National Safe Kids, every year 4.5 million children are injured at home—2 million seriously enough to require medical attention. Keeping a close eye on your children and taking simple preventative measures at your house (as well as at the grandparents') will keep your little ones from harm. Here are tips for making every room as child-safe as possible.

CRIB AND NURSERY SAFETY

■ Does the changing table have a safety belt to prevent falls?

■ Is the baby powder out of baby's reach during diaper changing?

■ Are changing supplies within your reach when baby is being changed?

■ Is there a carpet or a nonskid rug beneath the crib and changing table?

■ Are drapery and blind cords out of the baby's reach from the crib and changing table?

■ If you've purchased a new crib mattress, be sure to remove all plastic coverings, because these pose a suffocation hazard to your baby.

■ To reduce the risk of SIDS (sudden infant death syndrome), put your baby to sleep on his or her back in a crib with a firm, flat mattress and no soft bedding underneath.

■ Does the mattress in the crib fit snugly, without any gaps, so your child cannot slip in between the crack and the crib side?

■ Does the crib sheet fit just right? If it's too loose or too tight, it can come off and strangle or suffocate the baby.

■ Be sure the crib has no elevated corner posts or decorative cutouts in the end panels. Loose clothing can become snagged on these and strangle your baby.

■ The slats on the crib should be no more than 2⅜ inches apart. Widely spaced slats can trap an infant's head.

■ Are all screws, bolts, and hardware, including mattress supports, in place to prevent the crib from collapsing?

■ Check the crib for small parts and pieces that your child could choke on.

■ Have all crib gyms, hanging toys, and decorations removed from the crib by the time your baby can sit, or by five months, whichever comes first.

■ As soon as your baby can sit, lower the crib mattress so he or she can't fall out. When he or she can stand, set the mattress at its lowest position.

■ When your baby can pull to a standing position, remove toys, pillows, and stuffed animals that are large enough to be used as a step for climbing out.

■ Be sure the night-light is not near or touching drapes or a bedspread where it could start a fire. Buy only night-lights that do not get hot.

■ Is there a smoke detector in or near your child's bedroom?

■ Install window guards to prevent a child from falling out the window. Never place a crib, playpen, or other children's furniture near a window.

■ Be sure a toy box does not have a heavy, hinged lid that can trap your child. (It is safer with no lid at all.)

■ To keep the air moist, use a cool mist humidifier (not a vaporizer). Clean it frequently, and empty it when not in use to keep bacteria and mold from growing in the still water.

KITCHEN SAFETY

- Install cabinet locks on low cabinets and drawers that contain sharp knives and potentially toxic cleaning products.

- Place kitchen appliances away from the edges of counters. Be sure electrical appliance cords aren't dangling from countertops.

- Keep toddlers away from the stove at all times. Mark off a zone that he or she knows is not safe to enter.

- If stove knobs are within a child's reach, use protective covers to prevent turning.

- When cooking, turn pot handles toward the back of the stove, and use the back burners whenever possible.

- Keep counters clear of clutter.

- Place a pot or pan over a hot burner until the burner has cooled.

- Keep high chairs, chairs, and step stools away from counters and the stove.

- Store cookies and treats children might reach for far away from the stove area.

- Keep the kids out of the kitchen when you are frying.

- If possible, stow trash and recyclables in a locked cabinet or closet.

- Keep plastic bags, plastic wrap, and foil out of reach. Tie plastic bags in knots before storing or recycling them.

- Use placemats instead of a tablecloth so your child cannot pull the contents of the table down on top of him- or herself.

- Set your water heater to 120 degrees or cooler to prevent scalding from the kitchen faucet.

- Load silverware into the dishwasher with the handles facing up.

- Remove small magnets—potential choking hazards—from your fridge.

- Never hold a hot beverage while carrying your child, no matter how careful you plan to be.

- Clean up broken glass slivers with a damp, disposable cloth, then vacuum. Mop thoroughly before letting your children back into the area.

- Keep a working fire extinguisher handy.

BATHROOM SAFETY

- Be sure electrical appliances, such as blow-dryers, are unplugged, away from water, and out of a child's reach.

- Store hazardous items such as razors, scissors, and medicines out of a child's reach, preferably in a locked cabinet.

- Be sure all medications have childproof lids.

- Keep the toilet seat down and the door to the bathroom closed or gated. Or buy hinged toilet lid locks that clamp to the lip of the bowl.

- Place a nonskid mat or decals in the bathtub.

- Use a large, nonskid rug on the bathroom floor.

- Supervise your children's baths; don't use bath seats, which can tip.

- Test bathwater before putting your child in the tub.

- Toss a small hand towel over the top of a bathroom door when your child is using the rest room so it won't close completely. This way, little ones are less likely to lock themselves in.

LIVING AREAS AND BEDROOM SAFETY

- Secure unstable furniture such as bookshelves, entertainment centers, or dressers that could topple if a child pulls on them.

- Install cushioned corners on sharp corners of tables and other furniture with pointed edges.

- Move your TV, and other electronic equipment out of reach.

- Run electrical cords along baseboards, securing them to the floor when possible. Bind up any extra cord. Check regularly to be sure they're not frayed or overloaded.

- Install short cords on phones or secure the cords up high out of reach. Better still, use cordless phones. You eliminate the choking hazard and make yourself mobile, which means you never have to leave young kids unattended to answer the phone.

- Shorten long cords for blinds or draperies. Wrap them around wall brackets, wind them up, and tie the cords with a short string, or buy a cord wrap.

- Position your child's crib or bed away from drapery and electrical cords. Put night-lights at least three feet away from bedding and draperies to prevent fires.

- Keep pocket change and jewelry off the top of your dresser and out of reach.

- Light hallways and staircases to prevent falls.

- If you have older children whose toys have a lot of small pieces, buy organizing boxes with lids that close tightly so younger kids can't find them and choke on them.

- Install a screen or locked-glass enclosure on your fireplace. Remove irons and tools. Install screens around radiators, wood-burning stoves, and kerosene heaters.

- Cover fireplace hearths with protective cushioning.

- Test smoke alarms monthly, and replace batteries twice a year.

- Keep a list of emergency numbers (fire, police, pediatrician, poison control) by the phone.

SAFETY THROUGHOUT THE HOUSE

- Conduct a room-by-room inventory of potential dangers. Get down on all fours and view each room from the child's eye level. Be sure all potentially harmful items—cleaning products, perfumes, shoe polish, hair products, makeup, vitamins, mouthwash, medicine, alcoholic beverages, cigarettes, matches, and lighters—are out of a child's reach.

■ Keep potted houseplants in inaccessible locations; some are poisonous.

■ Put childproof covers on all electrical sockets.

■ Use childproof window latches.

■ Secure radiator covers and floor vents so a child cannot pull them off.

■ Affix decals at child-eye level to glass doors or windows that extend down to the floor.

■ Put slip-proof guards on uncarpeted stairs.

■ Use nonslip carpet tape or sticky matting under area rugs to hold them in place.

■ Use safety gates on rooms without doors to keep kids from wandering into dangerous areas.

■ Install safety gates at the top and bottom of stairs. Don't use a tension-mounted gate at the top of the stairs. If a child leans on it, it could become dislodged.

■ Put covers on doorknobs to rooms you don't want a child to enter. Or install hook-and-eye latches to keep doors closed.

■ Be sure you can unlock any door inside your home from the outside in case a child locks himself in a room.

■ Set chairs and tables by walls, not windows.

■ Consider installing plastic guards along the hinge side of frequently used interior doors to prevent pinched fingers.

■ To prevent choking, remove plastic end caps on doorstops or replace the stops with a one-piece design.

■ Lock doors of rooms children shouldn't be in by themselves.

■ Attach bells on exit doors to warn you if a child opens one.

■ Don't place furniture so a child is able to climb to a window or ledge.

OUTDOOR SAFETY

- Be sure any raised porch or deck has a railing and that the railing isn't wide enough for a child to climb through. If it is, cover the railing with Plexiglas, strong mesh, or lattice. Do the same for fences surrounding your property.

- Keep patio furniture away from the railings so a child cannot climb on them and fall over.

- Check wooden decks regularly for splinters.

- Install a latch on the door leading to your balcony or yard.

- Install a hook-and-eye latch on the outside of the gate to your yard so you can reach it but your child can't.

- Regularly check swings and other play equipment for rust, loose screws, splintering wood, or sharp edges.

- Be sure children's play equipment is securely anchored before use. Test it yourself to detect potentially unsafe structures.

- Put covers on swing chains to avoid caught fingers and torn clothes.

- Put wood chips, sand, or mulch under your swing set or play area. The deeper the fill, the safer your child will be in case of a fall. Be sure the fill extends out far enough that if your child is propelled from a swing, he will still land on a soft surface.

- Never take a child for a ride on a garden tractor or riding mower.

- Do not mow the lawn with a child nearby. The blade often kicks up sharp objects.

- Return gardening equipment to a locked shed or an inaccessible part of the garage immediately after its use.

- If your yard is not fenced off from the street, establish a safety zone along the front yard that your child knows to stay inside. Buy orange safety cones and teach your child not to go past them.

- Keep the play area clean of pet droppings. Keep cats out of the sandbox by covering it when not in use.

- Coil and return the garden hose to its hanger when not in use.

- String clotheslines out of your child's reach.

- Be sure wooden fences have rounded, well-sanded posts. See that a chain-link fence has no barbs sticking up.

- Teach your child to stay away from the barbecue grill.

- Get rid of highly poisonous or toxic plants growing in your back or front yard. Call your local poison-control center for a list of dangerous plants in your area.

- After a rainy period, remove any mushrooms or toadstools, because they could be poisonous.

- Store ladders out of reach, or secure them to the wall horizontally so they will not tempt your child to climb.

- Keep your car locked to prevent your child from climbing inside, activating the garage door opener, or knocking the car out of gear.

Finding Quality Child Care

Some working parents are fortunate enough to have flexible daytime schedules or to have their children enrolled in company-sponsored child care. But for many, child care continues to be an issue—one that's sometimes hard to feel good about. Guilt over leaving kids with "strangers" fuels the nagging concern, *Is this the best I can do for my child?*

What's important to recognize is that often, the answer is yes. In today's society, this is the economic reality for millions of families. So if arranging child care is a necessity for your household, realize that even if you can't be with your children twenty-four hours a day, you can ensure that they get the best care possible. Deciding which situation will best suit you and your child can seem like a daunting task. You'll have to consider factors such as the type of arrangement, your budget, and convenience. But taking a businesslike approach and breaking things down can help you with this important decision.

■ **Research your options.** Ask friends and co-workers for recommendations. Check out local churches, synagogues, and YMCAs. Consult the Yellow Pages under child care, day-care centers, and nanny services. Don't settle on one kind of care—in-home or day care—until you've examined all the options.

■ **List your requirements:**

☐ What hours will you be working?

☐ Will you work overtime?

☐ Who will be your designated backup if you or your spouse is traveling?

☐ What is your budget for child care?

☐ What do your children need? Do they have special interests that will be met?

☐ Is the day-care center close to your home or office?

☐ What about child care when the child is sick?

■ **Interview prospective sitters, nannies, or other child-care providers.** Ask questions that require detailed answers, including:

☐ Can you provide references? What did you do for those people?

☐ What will you and the children do during the day? Can you outline what a typical day would be like?

☐ What would you do in an emergency? Do you know CPR?

☐ Would you work on a trial basis (with pay) for a few days before I go back to work to see how it works out?

■ **Trust your instincts.** You'll sense whether an environment is the right one for your child.

■ **Be prepared for glitches.** Kids and nannies get sick. Take time to arrange a backup plan should your sitter be unavailable or your child not be able to attend day care.

Questions to Ask Every Day-Care Center

Before calling or visiting a day-care center or home-based day care, familiarize yourself with the state licensure regulations for these places. These are the state's requirements for everything from a caregiver's education to the day care's sanitation. (Go to www.FirstGov.gov to find your state's database.)

When you've narrowed your list to a few, do some quick phone interviews with prospective day-care personnel, taking notes on the answers. Ask:

☐ What ages do you care for?

☐ Do you have openings?

☐ What hours are you open? What happens if I'm late to pick up my child?

☐ What goals and philosophies shape the way you care for children?

☐ How many kids is each caregiver responsible for? (See the following box.)

☐ What are your caregivers' educational backgrounds? What experience have they had with children?

☐ What is your policy when a child become sick—mine or someone else's?

☐ What is your disciplinary policy?

☐ How do you handle medical emergencies?

☐ Can we visit without notice or participate in daily activities?

☐ Will you be willing to describe my child's day and answer any questions we have?

Follow up with visits to the most promising candidates. Look around and consider:

The Child-to-Caregiver Ratio

The National Association for the Education of Young Children recommends the following:

Birth–1 year: A maximum of eight children per two caregivers.

2–2.5 years: A maximum of twelve children per two caregivers.

2.5–3 years: A maximum of fourteen children per two caregivers.

3–5 years: A maximum of ten children per two caregivers.

☐ Do the children seem content?

☐ Do they have opportunities to learn and explore?

☐ Are both indoor and outdoor and age-appropriate activities provided?

☐ Does each child have a space for his or her personal items?

☐ Is every area childproofed?

☐ Are the routine and rules child-friendly?

☐ Is homework help available for older kids?

Finally, take your kids to visit the most promising candidates. Let them respond honestly about how they feel in each setting.

Is Your Child in Good Hands?

A great caregiver will:

- Honor your values.

- Be someone with whom you could be friends.

- Gladly answer questions about herself.

- Greet your kids.

- Show character you'd like your kids to learn.

- Offer a safe, simple routine.

- Explain rules in a firm, kid-friendly way.

- Give special attention when a child is ill or upset.

- Show and teach respect for people who are different.

- Encourage a child's good behavior with praise.

Getting Started

Once you've chosen a day-care center, consider starting to use it a week before you begin your job. This gives you and your child time to adjust.

■ Obviously like kids and encourage their individuality.

■ Talk to and hold babies.

■ Manage special needs without complaint.

■ Refer to children by their casual names (e.g., Randy instead of Randall).

■ Talk to your children, asking about their day and answering their questions.

■ Teach health habits such as washing hands after bathroom visits.

■ Pay more attention to your child than to you.

■ Encourage independence and skill-building, such as using good table manners, washing hands and face, picking up toys, etc.

■ Know when to offer help and when to let the child do for himself.

■ Be alert to your child's needs.

■ Won't tolerate children's bullying each other or calling each other names.

A poor caregiver will:

■ Raise her voice and use severe punishment—spanking, isolating children, withholding food.

■ Ignore your children.

■ Spend hours in front of the TV or on the phone.

■ Use negative language, saying "don't" frequently and threatening discipline unnecessarily.

■ Overlook bullying and bad behavior.

Field Trip Safety

Many preschools and day-care centers plan field trips for children. Before agreeing to let your child participate, ask the following questions:

■ Will there be continuous adult supervision on all trips?

■ When will parents be informed about the field trip—when it is, where they're going, and what they will do—so you can prepare your child and dress her appropriately?

■ Are there safety rules and behavior guidelines children will be expected to follow? (Review these with your child ahead of time.)

■ Will a licensed driver or bus company transport the kids?

■ What type of identification will children wear? (Tags should reveal only the group or school name, not the child's name. A stranger could lure a child by pretending to know his name.)

Information Your Baby-Sitter Must Know

Don't leave home without equipping your baby-sitter with this essential information in case of emergency.

PHONE NUMBERS
- ☐ Your cell phone or pager
- ☐ Where you will be
- ☐ A couple close friends, relatives, or neighbors
- ☐ Fire department
- ☐ Police department
- ☐ Poison Control
- ☐ Your pediatrician
- ☐ A nearby hospital

INSTRUCTIONS
- ☐ Guidelines for child's eating and drinking, including foods that are off-limits
- ☐ Dosage and time for any medications
- ☐ Nap- or bedtimes, and how to enforce them
- ☐ Activities your child likes
- ☐ Things he or she is not allowed to do when you're away
- ☐ TV limits and acceptable programs
- ☐ Disciplinary measures
- ☐ Instructions for using baby or other equipment
- ☐ Reminder not to open doors to strangers, and how to answer phone
- ☐ Sitter's guidelines for phone use, TV, drinking or smoking, and having visitors
- ☐ What to do in case of emergency

- [ ] Locations of fire and burglar alarms, first-aid supplies, fuse box, flashlights, and all entrances and exits

- [ ] In case sitter needs this info in an emergency, write down and post your address with clear directions to your home

> You can download and print medical consent forms and baby-sitter information forms at www.familymanager.com.

MEDICAL CONSENT FORMS

Provide a consent form in case your child requires medical attention. The form should include:

- [ ] Your child's name

- [ ] His or her date of birth

- [ ] Your insurance carrier and policy number

- [ ] Doctor's names and phone numbers

- [ ] Vital medical history, such as allergies and chronic conditions

- [ ] This statement: "Any licensed physician, dentist, or hospital may give necessary emergency medical service to my child, [your child's name], at the request of the person bearing this consent form."

- [ ] Both parents' signatures

Is a Baby-Sitting Co-Op Right for You?

Many moms have found a barter system a superior means of child care. By forming a co-op with other busy parents, you'll be able to handle more easily those middle-of-the-day appointments as well as evenings out. And because no money changes hands, it's always affordable!

WHY THEY WORK

- Children stay with your friends, who are parents themselves. You can rest easy, knowing your child is with experienced, loving adults.

- Your kids see these outings as a treat: Instead of being "left behind" by Mom and Dad, they get to play with other kids—and other kids' toys.

- Because you exchange baby-sitting, you need never feel guilty about asking someone to sit. Everyone benefits, so everyone gladly contributes.

HOW TO START A BABY-SITTING CO-OP

- Make a list of other local, like-minded families who might be interested.

- Have a meeting to organize prospective participants to discuss membership requirements, whether you'll elect officers, the size of the co-op, how often you will meet, dues for supplies, general guidelines for managing emergencies, what to do in case of a child's sudden illness, discipline issues, how to handle late pickups, and adding or eliminating members.

- Set up your exchange system. Use tickets or points. For example, "charge" one ticket or point (or more) for baby-sitting one child per hour. If you use points, you'll need a secretary to record points accrued and spent for each co-op member.

- Arrange for rotating members to manage secretarial tasks: typing and distribution of co-op rules, meeting information, and medical consent forms.

- Set up a personal record-keeping system for each child. This includes every child's food allergies or special medical needs, pediatrician's name and phone number, what hospital you prefer, your insurance information, emergency contacts, and a notarized permission slip for medical attention.

Sharing a Nanny

My friend Michele Stephens, a dual-career mom, came up with a creative, guilt-reducing child-care alternative for her family. Both she and her husband dreaded the idea of dragging their daughter out of bed every morning and making sure they had packed enough diapers, extra clothes, and food or drink for each day. They much preferred the idea of their child staying home, so they looked into nanny agencies but found them much too expensive. Then they began to brainstorm: What about sharing a nanny with a family or two? Michele's house would be the home base, and the nanny could care for all the children there.

Next, they located interested families. She recommends looking for six qualities in potential nanny-sharers:

- **Similar values and expectations.** You need to view discipline and right and wrong the same way.

- **Similar schedules.** If you have to be at work at 8 A.M., it won't work if the other parents go in at 6 A.M.

- **Willingness to sign a contract.** By signing a contract, all parties are making a commitment.

- **Dependability.** It's important to find parents who will pay on time for their share of the nanny, who will pick up their children on schedule, and who will follow through on other terms of the agreement.

- **Good Health.** All children share colds, but it's good to inquire about the health of the child and the family in general. Also, if your family has pets, the children coming into your home shouldn't have allergies.

- **The other kids' personalities.** Are they going to be good playmates for your child? Age, sex, interests, and temperament all play a part. Children of the same age and sex typically are a good match; however, children can learn a lot from older and younger children.

This solution takes care of several issues. Your child gets to stay in her own home: She naps in her own bed, plays with her own toys, and romps in her own yard. Second, a nanny—a trained, licensed child-care professional—becomes affordable. And third, kids without siblings have other children to play with.

Play Groups

Starting a play group (in which parents take turns watching one another's kids) is a great way to buy yourself some child-free time for doctors' appointments, shopping, and relaxing. To start a group that really works, meet with other interested parents first and together figure out:

- **Who will join.** A group of four to five kids of a similar age is optimal for the under-four set, especially if there is only one parent on duty. (Be sure you get every parent's address, phone number, and emergency phone number.)

- **What the schedule will be.** Two hours is plenty for toddlers and preschoolers to play in a group. You might allow fifteen minutes to get settled, thirty minutes of a preplanned craft or activity, fifteen minutes for a snack, forty-five minutes of outdoor or free play, and fifteen minutes of rest while listening to a book or music.

- **When the group will meet.** Once a week? On what day? Mornings tend to work best because young children are less tired before lunch and more willing to cooperate with other kids and try new things.

- **Where you'll meet.** In the host's home? At a local playground?

- **How to handle fights, separation anxiety, and other issues.**

Put everything in writing, and be sure each parent has a copy of the guidelines before the children get together. When it's your turn to entertain all the tots, plan ahead so the supplies and snacks you'll need for hosting are within easy reach.

Home Alone but Not Lonely—or Bored

Knowing that your child is coming home to an empty house after school isn't always easy for you or her. Even if you're confident that she's capable of looking after herself, both the parent and child benefit when you establish certain routines and house rules. And finding little ways to let your child know that you care—even when you can't be there—also goes a long way. Here are some ideas on how to help your home-alone kid:

- Surprise your child with words of encouragement, praise, or affection by jotting them down on sticky-notes left on the bathroom mirror, refrigerator door, TV or computer screen, or his or her bedroom door.

- Fill out and post a "Parent Locator and Emergency Number" list. You can download this form at www.family manager.com.

- Put a list of snack ideas on the fridge. To keep appliance use to a minimum, suggest only no-cook snack ideas.

- Put a small emergency pack (an extra house key, quarters for a phone, list of phone numbers, and folded money for emergency transportation) in your child's backpack.

- Develop a family code word. If an unfamiliar person has to pick up your child at school, she can use the code to show she's safe. This word can also mean "Help" if your child must call you in a frightening situation.

- Stock your cabinet with medical supplies and teach your child basic first aid. Find out if your local hospital offers courses for kids.

- Plan some creative activities your child can do alone. Be sure you have all the supplies needed for the projects.

- Reduce the number of hours your child spends at home alone by signing her up for an after-school sports activity, a cooking class, or other regularly scheduled classes such as dance or tennis.

Establish Home-Alone Rules

Consider these issues, and post your rules in an easy-to-see place, such as the refrigerator door.

- Under what circumstances are kids allowed to use the stove (if any)?

- Are friends allowed to visit? Must your child ask permission first? Is having more than one friend over okay? What about friends of the opposite sex?

- What chores should be tackled each day, and by whom? Post a list, and check in via phone or e-mail to remind kids.

- Decide what programs and how much TV is permissible. Have kids track TV time and report what they watched. (Also see Internet Safety, page 127).

- Are your kids allowed to go anywhere after school? Where, and how will they let you know where they are?

Help Your Child Succeed in School

Acquiring the skills needed to excel in school starts well before your child ever sets foot in a classroom. By involving your children in simple, creative tasks and fun games designed to enhance learning, you'll be giving them one of the greatest gifts: a love of learning.

YOUNGER KIDS

- Read to young children daily. This helps them develop listening and observation skills, and it stimulates imagination.

- Choose books with story lines they can relate to: the addition of a sibling, going on a trip, visiting a doctor or dentist, etc.

- Before reading a new book to young children, tell them the title and ask what they think the story might be about. When you have almost finished reading the book, ask your children to make up an ending to the story.

- Link reading books with television programs. If your child watches a show about birds, check out a book at the library on the same subject, and read it together.

- Establish a reading corner for your child set up with a comfy chair, good reading light, and a basket of books.

- Teach young children to follow directions; it is one of the most important skills they need in school. When showing children how to perform a new task or skill, model each part of the job. Then let them participate with you until they can do the task alone. And remember to give instructions one at a time, followed by doing that part of the task.

- When taking preschool children to the bank, bakery, cleaners, post office, or service station, tell them about the kinds of work the people do and why their services are needed.

> "You cannot teach a child to take care of himself unless you will let him try to take care of himself. He will make mistakes; and out of these mistakes will come his wisdom." —Henry Ward Beecher

- Talk about sounds with your child: workers repairing the street, a train whistle, dogs barking, cash register ringing, or birds chirping. For fun, try to mimic the sounds together.

- Young children need to build with blocks, play with clay, put together puzzles, and do simple exercises such as bending, crawling, hopping, stretching, or walking. This helps them develop their large and small motor skills and prepares them to learn tasks that require physical dexterity at school.

- Teach art education on the go. Look for shapes and lines while you're in the car. Highway stripes are straight; rooftops have angles; roads are curved; traffic signals are dots; open manholes are circles. Preschoolers can learn to identify shapes by looking at road signs.

- Teach children letters of the alphabet by having them look for all the A's or B's on a magazine page. As the child finds the letter, she can color it with a highlighter.

- Make an alphabet book. In a spiral notebook, write each letter of the alphabet on different pages. Look through magazines, and help your child find pictures that begin with each letter. Cut out the pictures and paste them in the notebook.

- Make up stories that stimulate your children's imagination. When you're in the car or around the dinner table, have one family member start the story and each person after add more to the adventure. For example:

Dad: There once was a dog named Banjo who lived . . .

Mom: In a small town in Colorado. He was a medium-size dog . . .

Child One: With black-and-white spots. Everyone loved Charlie because . . .

Child Two: He had rescued many people who had fallen into snow drifts that winter. But one afternoon . . .

- Assign your child to be the daily weather reporter. His job is to learn the weather each day from a local radio or television station or the Internet and report to the family so you can plan the day's activities. Check the thermometer to see if he was correct about the temperature high for the day.

Teaching Tidiness

I remember days when my child's room reminded me of a spiritual sanctuary—when I entered, there was no other choice but to walk the straight and narrow way and pray I could make it to the other side. Early on, kids should get in the habit of picking up their rooms before bed and cleaning up their rooms before school. It saves stress later in the day, and everyone appreciates a tidy room where he can find everything easily. For best results, make this chore as easy as possible:

■ Every night before bed, start a routine of playing "What's Not in Its Home?" Together, search the room to find toys and belongings that are out of place and put them in their "homes."

■ Simplify bed-making. Set your child's bed slightly away from the wall. Use a comforter instead of a bedspread.

■ Create storage areas they can reach. Put most frequently used items in the lowest, easiest-access places.

■ Divide kids' closets into two parts: one for hanging clothes and one for shelves. Have two rods on the hanging side: a high rod for out-of-season and seldom-worn clothes and a child-level rod. Keep a small step stool in the closet for kids to reach higher shelves.

■ If your kids share a closet, paint each half of the rod a different color to prevent bickering.

■ Keep a small laundry basket in the closet for easy collection of dirty clothes.

■ If you have the wall space, hang pegs or hooks at child level for pajamas, backpacks, hats, etc.

■ Don't stuff drawers so full that kids can't remove items without making a mess. Regularly remove outgrown clothes.

■ Buy drawer organizers or use empty shoe boxes to divide socks, tights, and underwear.

ELEMENTARY-AGE KIDS

- Encourage children to read for pleasure and always have a book "in progress." Praise them regularly, and show interest in what they're reading by asking questions about the story and the characters. Offer rewards for reading.

- Encourage exploration. If your child asks why an animal behaves a certain way or why stars twinkle, make it a point to research it together on the Internet or go to the library and find out.

- Plant a small flower, herb, or vegetable garden together. Use plant catalogs to guide your choices. Read the directions to find out planting and care requirements.

- Appoint your child to be scorekeeper during a miniature golf game. Ask him or her to figure the average strokes for each player.

- Provide your children with the opportunity to do creative projects they show interest in, such as drawing, sewing, building models, caring for animals, learning simple geology, or working on mechanical projects.

- Help your child submit pictures, poems, riddles, or stories to children's magazines. They might get published.

- Keep a good dictionary and thesaurus handy. When your children read a word they don't know or hear an unfamiliar word on TV, teach them to look it up.

- Put old magazines to good use. Give two or more children a list of twenty-five things to hunt for, such as a boy, girl, car, flowers, a flag, or a horse. Have them tear the items out of the magazine. Allow twenty minutes to find all the items. The one who finds the most wins.

- Build your vocabulary as a family: Learn a new word every morning at the breakfast table. You can buy daily calendars with unusual or unfamiliar words; they also give the definition, a pronunciation guide, and a sentence to show how the word is used. Versions of these word calendars are available for older and younger children.

- Help your child learn handy skills. Repair a bike, take apart a small appliance, or build a simple piece of furniture together.

- Enroll your children in enrichment classes such as art, dance, drama, music, or science. These courses are often available for free or for a nominal fee through city parks and recreation departments, junior colleges, and YMCAs.

- Take your child to programs that complement a subject he or she is studying in school. For example, a civic theater, high school, or college might present a play or a musical your child is learning about in class. A planetarium might offer a course about the moon, which will make science studies come alive.

- Engage in stimulating discussions at the dinner table. Ask each family member to learn one thing every day to share at dinner.

- Have your child help plan menus and assist with grocery shopping and cooking. Encourage him to plan nutritional meals by reading the labels to compare fat and sugar content.

- Ask your child to research on the Internet your state department of tourism for lists of events in your area and maps of nearby places to visit. Let her plan a family outing.

- Before going on a car trip, look at a map and write the names of towns, rivers, and historical sites you will pass. During the drive, have kids mark each item and count off the miles.

- Teach your child how to read the car's odometer. On trips, he or she can figure out how many miles you have traveled and the average gas mileage.

- Find out your state bird, flower, and tree. If you plan to visit another state, look up the facts about that state in the encyclopedia.

"For the mother is and must be, whether she knows it or not, the greatest strongest and most lasting teacher her children have." —Hannah Whitall Smith

Starting School: Diminishing School Daze for First-Timers

Starting school is a major life change for kids. You can make the transition as smooth as possible by visiting the school beforehand, as well as introducing new routines and activities prior to the start of school:

- When you visit the school with your child, show him or her what activities will happen there; go over the names of new people; find out where the classroom will be and where the rest rooms are located. If possible, get a class list with phone numbers so you can arrange a few playdates with classmates before school starts.

- A week or so before the first day, implement schedule changes in household routines. Get up, get dressed, and eat breakfast as you will when school begins.

- Walk together to the bus stop or school a few times. Review safety rules and any after-school pickup arrangements. Remind your child never to go home with anyone else or get in a car with a stranger. (Don't write your child's name in large letters on his or her backpack or school bag; a stranger might fool a child into thinking he's a friend by calling the child's name.)

- Make a special day of buying school supplies and a first-day outfit.

- Be sure your child is comfortable with using a public bathroom. Remind him or her to always wash hands.

- Have your child practice using a lunch box or carrying a cafeteria tray of food.

- Plan to spend a few extra minutes before dropping off your child on the first day. Be sensitive; even a confident child can get stressed in a new situation.

Buy "fast" clothes—shoes with Velcro fasteners, tagless T-shirts, and shirts with ample openings for easy slipping over the head. Buttons, snaps, zippers, and shoelaces slow kids down.

Back to School: It's a Big Deal

Before school starts, plan a special family dinner to kick off the academic year. Serve favorite summer foods. Have each family member say what he or she learned this summer and what was most memorable. Toast the end of summer and begin to anticipate the new school year.

Pass out paper and pencils. Spend a few minutes writing down individual goals for the year (Mom and Dad, too). Place these papers in a file folder and review them in January and at the end of the school year.

■ Celebrate the moment! Take pictures at home of your child in his or her first-day outfit.

A Morning Exit Routine

Every family has experienced it: The school bus is coming down the block, Mom's meeting at the office starts in twenty minutes, and briefcase and backpack items are scattered all over the house. Once out of the house, Dad wonders if, in all the haste, he set the burglar alarm—or even locked the door.

> "The future is something which everyone reaches at the rate of sixty minutes an hour, whatever he does, whoever he is."
> —C. S. Lewis

Weekday mornings don't have to be a struggle. Gathering all necessary items the night before and creating an exit routine checklist means everyone can face the day with confidence and calm.

Kill panic with preparation! Use this Exit Checklist list to get you started:

KIDS
- ☐ Lunch box/meal card
- ☐ Textbooks
- ☐ Notebook(s), homework
- ☐ Signed permission slips
- ☐ Library books
- ☐ Notes for teachers
- ☐ House key
- ☐ Gym clothes
- ☐ Rain gear/outerwear
- ☐ Emergency money
- ☐ Musical instrument
- ☐ Other _____

MOM AND DAD
- ☐ Cleaning
- ☐ Bank deposit
- ☐ Library books
- ☐ Letters/packages to mail
- ☐ Lights and appliances off
- ☐ Answering machine on
- ☐ Frozen food out to thaw
- ☐ Doors locked
- ☐ Briefcase
- ☐ Car keys
- ☐ Purse
- ☐ Videos or DVDs to return
- ☐ Security system activated
- ☐ Other _____

(Print an Exit Checklist at www.familymanager.com to post near your door.)

Be Sensitive to Your Child's Learning Style

Kids may be primarily auditory, visual, and/or kinesthetic (hands-on) learners. To determine your children's dominant learning style, think about whether they talk about what they see (visual), what they hear (auditory), or if they say, "Show me" (kinesthetic). Watch them play: Do they watch or read to get information, listen attentively, or want to do it with their hands?

Understand that a primarily auditory learner will function better in a noisy atmosphere than a visual learner will. A visual learner needs to write down information and take notes. She also likes colorful illustrations and lots of pictures. A hands-on learner likes to feel things and communicate by touching. He's more fidgety by nature; breaking his homework into short segments with an activity in between will help.

LISTENING AND LEARNING

A tape player is a great learning tool for children who are auditory learners or who have difficulty reading. Here are some ways a recorder can be used:

- Have your child record his or her report before writing it. Then listen to the tape, and take down the report on paper.

- Record reading assignments for your children, such as a story or a chapter from a textbook. They can listen to the recording and follow along in the book. This way your children can check what they're hearing against

Become a Better Test-Taker!

Help your children learn to study effectively for tests. Encourage them to:

- Review notes soon after class.

- Color-code essential information with a highlighter in textbooks (if they own them). It also helps to highlight class notes. This makes it easier to review the important points.

- Ask the teacher what a test will cover if they're unsure about it.

- Save old tests to use as study guides.

- Study with several other students to review material before a test.

- Study according to their biological clocks. (When is each child's best time, early morning or evening?)

- For optimal retention, commit information to memory when they're rested.

- Learn how to use memory strategies, such as acronyms, key words, linking ideas, and rhyming.

- Proofread papers before turning them in, and use a dictionary as a quick way to check words for errors if not using a computer.

what's being read. They can listen to the recording several times to reinforce learning and improve reading skills.

- Ask the teacher for permission to use a tape recorder in class. Many children find it helpful to hear the lecture and assignment more than once.

- Encourage children who don't enjoy reading or don't read well to listen to stories on tape. Many local libraries offer tapes of classical literature as well as fun stories for young children. Listen to books on tape or CD while you're in the car, or let them listen to stories before bed.

End-of-the-School-Day Routines

Parents and kids alike need some time and space to recover from the day's stresses and accomplish days'-end tasks as efficiently and stress-free as possible. Here are some ways to promote peaceful evening hours:

- Give everyone time to rest and acclimate before beginning end-of-the-day activities. Change into comfortable clothes and spend a little time relaxing—even if it's only for a few minutes. Turn off your telephone, cell phone, pager, and television. Disconnect with the world so you can connect with yourself and your family.

- If you can't be home when kids arrive, be sure the caretaker shows interest in their day by listening to them describe how things went and asking questions that draw them out. You can also leave notes

---

When to Be Present

Many dual-career and single parents can't attend every school function. Only you can decide which ones are most important to you and your child. Here's a list of possibilities to get you started:

- The drop-off and pickup on the first day of school

- Academic meetings the school administration and teachers expect parents to attend

- Homecoming talent show

- Holiday programs

- One field trip during the year

- The science or art fair in which your child is a participant

- Any concert, assembly, or performance in which your child has a significant role

- Parents' open house

- Athletic games as possible in which your child participates

- Graduation or another important end-of-the-year celebration

If you can't attend an important event, call a relative or close friend to stand in for you. If possible, have someone videotape the event so your whole family can enjoy it together later.

for your children. Write a week's worth at one time and leave them in the same place each day.

■ Set an evening routine. Ours involved eating dinner and cleaning the kitchen together, then hitting the homework. The kids taped TV programs they didn't want to miss. We chose to keep afternoons free for ball practice, playing, and errand-running. Only if one's study load increased, or one's grades started slipping, did we insist on homework in the afternoons. However you assign your time, be sure to include a ten-minute hand of cards, walk with the dog, work on a puzzle—something fun the family can do together.

■ Establish that school is your children's "career" and is equally important to yours. When they see how you value their work, they will, too. Everyone should do "homework" together: kids do their schoolwork while Mom and Dad sort mail, read, or work quietly on a project. The TV and stereos should stay off.

■ Ask kids to decide what they'll wear and set out clothes the night before. (Pack away all clothing that doesn't fit, and put away out-of-season items to simplify decisions.) Have them put school gear in a designated place so they won't have to play hide-and-seek for books or gym shorts in the morning.

■ Set a specific time for younger children to bathe, brush their teeth, and go to bed so they'll have a sense of daily rhythm. Although they might stay up later on the weekends, don't alter the schedule greatly if you want the school-day routine to be easy to maintain.

■ Anticipate bedtime distractions. Make sure kids go to the bathroom before going to bed. Put a glass of water by the bed of a child who frequently needs a drink. Provide a night-light or flashlight for children who tend to be frightened of the dark.

■ Enforce a "lights out" time by installing a timer on kids' lights. Let them read or listen to books on tape until the light goes out.

Bring Back the Family Dinner Hour

Eating dinner together as a family is a simple way to nourish and nurture children, but it's also important in building strong family bonds. Studies show that kids who eat dinner together with their families on a regular basis do better in school and are less likely to do drugs than their peers.

■ **Cook smart and simple.** Come up with a list of your family's favorite dinner menus. Pick six to seven meals that you can prepare in less than thirty minutes, and always keep needed ingredients on hand. Don't let complicated recipes ruin your resolve. Remember, it's more important to eat together than to eat elaborate meals.

■ **Rely on teamwork.** Assign mealtime tasks by age, skill level, and time availability. Ask younger children to help clear the table or set the table, for example, or have everyone in charge of clearing his own plate after dinner. It's good for kids to realize that meals don't just magically appear on the table!

■ **Build respect with house rules.** Hold a family meeting and set some common house rules about acceptable behaviors in the household and at the dinner table (see House Rules, page 59, and Manners, page 115).

■ **Use a smart shopping list.** I created an envelope that serves as my menu planner, grocery list, and coupon holder. It's always available for easy reference, so I don't have to reinvent the wheel week after week. (The Family Manager Grocery Planner is available on my website.)

■ **Clean up as you go.** Fill your sink with warm water and soap while preparing dinner. Soak pans and utensils while you're eating for quicker cleanup later.

■ **Focus on family.** Cut off the outside world, turn off the television, and don't answer the phone during dinnertime. Get quality conversations started by asking each family member to share the best thing that happened to them that day.

Homework Hints for Success

■ Show interest in your children's schoolwork, and display it on a bulletin board. Look at their textbooks and ask them what they enjoy learning about the most. Ask them what subjects are difficult for them and where they need help. Let them know you struggled with some subjects, too.

■ Teach kids to make a list of what they need to accomplish, then prioritize what they need to do first.

■ Help kids guess how long it will take them to finish homework, then let them time themselves. They will learn about time management.

■ Help them understand the importance of doing advance work, such as making sure their sports uniforms are clean and getting all equipment together in plenty of time before the game.

■ Teach your children to multitask while watching TV. They can clean out their notebooks or backpacks or organize art or office supplies during their favorite shows.

■ Model the behavior you want them to embrace. If they see you procrastinating about a project you need to tackle, don't expect them to behave differently. Talk about how you can learn together to be better managers of time.

■ When they get older, encourage kids to keep their own calendar notebook or use a computer calendar program where they can record important facts and dates.

■ Help them break a big task—writing a book report or preparing for the science fair—into small segments.

■ Create homework incentive programs. Children earn points toward an award by doing homework on the day it is assigned, completing it on time, and having a good attitude.

■ Discuss how to do special projects or papers with your children before they start them. Help your children think through the following: What does the teacher want? What items do you need to complete the project? What is available? What other resources do I need to check into? Help them make a list of needed steps if necessary.

■ See what resources are available before starting projects and reports. Your public library often houses special collections on various subjects. It might also carry clippings or memorabilia on local history. Grandparents might have an antique, old books, newspapers, or photographs that could be used for an interesting report. If a child has to write a paper on the judicial system, arrange for him to interview a lawyer. If you have a hobby, your child might be able to use it as a source for a project.

■ Study along with your kids. One mom I know enrolled in an algebra refresher course at the local college so she could help her freshman son with his studies.

■ Stress the importance of neatness. Teachers are influenced by the way work looks. If your children's handwriting is poor, encourage them to do the best they can. Reward practicing penmanship at home. When possible, let your children do their work on a computer.

■ Talk about the grades your child brings home and what was required to earn them on different assignments.

A Work Space Works Wonders

Having a designated space for homework gives a child a sense of routine. Each child needs his or her own area in which to do homework. Set up a good study environment. Some children like to be alone and quiet, while others prefer to be near people. If they don't have desks, give kids specific areas on the dining room table or other surface.

Supply whatever each needs to do his or her work. Store everything your children need in one spot so they don't waste time scavenging for highlighters or binder paper. We kept office supplies on hand for homework projects, such as construction, lined, and plain white paper; different colors of felt pens and pencils; folders for reports; and poster board.

BASICS:

☐ Desk or other flat working surface (the kitchen table is fine if family respects quiet study time)

☐ Comfortable chair (for certain projects, your child might need to spread out on the floor)

- ☐ Good lighting

- ☐ File folders, labels, and a filing box or crate

- ☐ In/out boxes

- ☐ Class list with phone numbers (to call other students if your child forgets an assignment)

- ☐ Computer (if possible)

- ☐ Calendar (to plan long-term school projects)

SCHOOL SUPPLIES:

- ☐ Ballpoint pens
- ☐ Blank paper
- ☐ Calculator
- ☐ Colored pencils
- ☐ Compass
- ☐ Construction paper
- ☐ Erasers
- ☐ Folders with pockets (in various colors)
- ☐ Glue
- ☐ Graph paper
- ☐ Highlighter pens in various colors

- ☐ Index cards
- ☐ Marketers
- ☐ Notepad
- ☐ Paper clips
- ☐ Pencils
- ☐ Pencil sharpener
- ☐ Poster board
- ☐ Ruler
- ☐ Scissors
- ☐ Special notebook (in which to write homework assignments)
- ☐ Stapler and staples
- ☐ Tape

Television as a Teacher

Television, if used properly, can be a useful learning tool. When viewed in moderation, with guidance from watchful parents, TV can help kids become critical thinkers.

Make the most of your television set by heeding these tips:

- Set a limit on viewing per week. Educators suggest a maximum of ten hours weekly for elementary-school-age kids.

- Help children become aware of misleading special effects used on TV.

- Don't channel surf; select specific programs from the TV schedule each week.

- Encourage kids to watch shows that have positive role models; that teach them cooperation, interaction, and appreciation of other cultures; and that excite their imaginations.

- Teach children that aggression is not the way to solve conflict.

- Keep the TV off during homework time.

- Encourage kids to think about and even question what they're watching rather than just taking it in.

- If possible, preview programs. Okay the ones you think are suitable.

- When your children want to see a program you're unsure about, watch it together. Then discuss it:

How would you rate this show on a scale from one to ten?
What was the program's message?
Could you identify with any of the characters?
Did you feel this program portrayed life as it really is?
What would you have done to help any of the characters?
Was there anything in the show you did not agree with?
What in the show uplifted you or inspired you to be a better person?
Was this program worth the time you spent on it?

Get Me to the Church
(Ball Game, School Play, or Dance Class) on Time!

Had it with conflicting schedules for after-school activities? It might be time to form a car pool. Here's how.

1. GATHER A GROUP

- Find other parents who might also need to car pool. Skip those who might let their teenagers do the driving for them.

- Let your child react to each of the names of car pool candidates—see if he or she is comfortable with them.

- Check out the candidates' driving competency.

2. SET GROUND RULES

- Get the group together to discuss guidelines.

- Find out and share what the school's security procedures are for kids being dropped off.

- Be sure drivers have adequate insurance to cover kids in their care.

- Decide who can drive and who can cover for each driver in case of illness. Make a firm list.

- Decide whether you want to commit to daily or weekly driving duties.

- Distribute calendars, then work on a schedule together.

- Talk about potential scheduling conflicts and how to handle emergencies.

- Make one master calendar and put someone in charge of it. That person should copy the master calendar and distribute it.

> "It seems to me I spent my life in car pools, but you know, that's how I kept track of what was going on." —**Barbara Bush**

3. GET INFORMATION

- Have drivers write down names, addresses, and phone numbers.

- Create a master phone list and distribute.

- Have parents write down their children's essential information and distribute. Each driver should have this for each child.

- Keep this information in the car in case of medical or other emergency.

- Each driver should fill out this information for him- or herself as well and distribute it.

- Talk about whether to get permission forms or notarized medical releases for each child to carry in the car.

- Decide whether to copy each child's health-insurance card and distribute it to each driver.

4. SPELL OUT SAFETY RULES

- Urge drivers to carry cell phones but not try to talk on them while they drive.

- Encourage drivers to store maps in their cars.

- Agree to keep number of children in a car to the number of seat belts available.

- Make a policy of not starting the car until everyone is belted in.

- Make an agreement to keep cars in safe working order.

- Consider stocking each car with a first-aid kit.

- Be sure cars have jacks, jumper cables, spare tires, emergency flat-tire inflator product, and so on.

- Discuss child car seats and decide how to pass these around.

- Discuss and make policies on:

    - Kids sitting only in the backseat

    - Eating and drinking in the car

    - Driver counting kids before starting the car

    - Keeping doors locked and windows rolled up while car is moving

    - Never leaving children alone in the car

    - What to do if no one is home when a child is to be dropped off.

    - Disciplining unruly kids (The best policy is to stop the car until kids have calmed down.)

5. GET STARTED!

- Keep kids informed about who is driving each day.

■ If someone must use a substitute, he or she should let all the parents know of the change.

(You can print a car pool form at www.familymanager.com.)

Making Sick Days Better Days

It never fails. The morning your Daily Hit List seems endless will be the day a child gets sick. If you find yourself feeling frustrated because you can't accomplish all you'd planned, remember that the hours spent beside a child's sickbed or the tedious days enduring a lengthy siege of the flu can be turned into warm, caring moments. In the long run, your children will appreciate your tender care—and remember it long after they're grown—more than a spotless kitchen or a clean closet.

Use this sick-day plan to help you keep frustration to a minimum:

■ Be prepared. Have numbers handy for your doctor and pharmacy. When you call your doctor, be prepared with this information:

Child's temperature
Symptoms—headaches, pulling at ears, sore throat, vomiting, diarrhea, stomachache, rash, unusual sleep patterns
Medication you've given so far

■ Keep your medicine cabinet well stocked with necessary over-the-counter medications and medical supplies.

■ Create a special box that you keep on a high closet shelf and get down only on sick days. For younger kids, fill it with activity and coloring books, crayons, stickers, a pad of paper, watercolors, glue, construction paper, pieces of ribbon and yarn, and magazines with lots of pictures (for cutting up). Older kids might enjoy a model or craft project to work on.

■ Designate a spot in your pantry for "sick foods," such as chicken noodle soup, clear soda pop, flavored gelatin, and soda crackers. Tell family members these items are for sick days only.

"A mother is completely fatigued. She has been telling her friends for weeks that there is nothing left in her and then a child falls ill and needs her. Week after week, night after night, she stands by and never thinks of being tired."

—Harry Emerson Fosdick

- Be sensitive to what your child prefers when he or she is sick, whether to be left alone in bed or in the middle of things on the family room sofa.

- Create a fresh atmosphere for a child with a lengthy illness. Put on clean pillowcases and let fresh air into the room daily.

- For a prolonged illness, send your child a small gift each day through the mail—new markers, a pack of gum, a package of flower seeds, or a small book. Watching for the mail carrier will be something fun to do each day.

- Buy or make a large-size bib with the words "I Feel Better" painted or monogrammed on it. This is a big help when a younger child is attempting to sip broth or eat a meal on a bed tray.

- Flavored gelatin is more fun for kids when it's prepared in a 9 × 12-inch cake pan. Use cookie cutters to cut fun figures for your patient to eat. Dry toast also tastes better when it's cut into shapes.

- Brighten your sick child's room with colored crepe paper and a cheery poster taped to the ceiling.

Call ahead before you take a sick child to an appointment at the doctor's office because doctors tend to run late with appointments. Ask the receptionist for a realistic arrival time so you won't have to spend unnecessary time in the waiting room.

Create a Medical Bag filled with books, games, stickers, and other fun objects for your child to enjoy only when visiting the doctor.

If you have two or more children, arrange to leave the well kids with another mom or caretaker while you take your ill child to the doctor. That way, you can focus your full attention on your sick youngster as you wait. Then return the favor when your friend's children have doctor's appointments.

- Encourage family members to slip get-well cards under the patient's door or put them on a meal tray. See if your child's class will make get-well cards if he or she will be out of school for a long period.

- Call your child's teacher and ask if you can pick up schoolwork. Encourage your child to get as much schoolwork done as possible while at home.

- Play board games or work puzzles. Read new or old favorite books aloud. Get out family albums and pictures to look at together. Tell your child stories about what he or she did when younger. Reminisce about a favorite vacation, including the attractions and the highlights of the trip.

■ Plan a special outing together for when the child is better.

Important Subjects Your Kids Won't Learn in School

Some of the most important aspects of our children's education are about things they won't learn in school. Our homes must be the classrooms, and we are the teachers. Here are six important values to teach your kids.

1. Responsibility. Children aren't born knowing they should treat possessions—their own or someone else's—with care. They learn quickly, though, when you let them suffer the consequences of poor choices. Let them know that if they leave their bikes in the rain, toys in the yard, and coats at school, and these items are broken, destroyed, or stolen, you will not automatically replace them. When they break (even accidentally) another child's toy, make your child, as the responsible party, help pay for a replacement.

2. Productivity. Chores—they might not want 'em, but they need 'em. Even two-year-olds can fold towels and pick up toys. Toddlers probably won't fold the towels as neatly as you'd like, but that's okay. It's more important that they learn to be productive. Even if someone cleans your

> *"In automobile terms, the child supplies the power but the parents have to do the steering."*
> —Dr. Benjamin Spock

house, you should require your kids to do household chores. Children need to see themselves as productive contributors to the welfare of the home, because they benefit from living there.

As kids grow older and getting an allowance becomes an attractive possibility, you have an excellent opportunity to teach them that getting money is related to working. They get paid for doing part of the family's work and, therefore, get a portion of the family's money. If children choose not to do part of the family's work, they don't get a portion of the family's money. It's that simple.

We made the decision to never do anything or buy anything on a regular basis

Rewarding Kids for Work

There are many schools of thoughts about kinds of reward for work. I tend to stay away from monetary rewards for everyday chores. But when the boys did an above-and-beyond-the-normal-call-of-duty job, i.e., put insulation in the attic to cut down our utility bill, paint a room, or scrub mildew off the ceiling of a big porch, we paid them. Another exception was our annual garage sale, in which the whole family participates and takes a share of the profits to use as they see fit. I think kids are better motivated in the long run by seeing that everybody working together makes home a happier place to be.

When the boys were younger, I was known to reward extra chores with chits, gold stars, things like that, which could eventually be traded in for things they wanted. I also tried to schedule "fun" errands after a day of hard work, so that washing and vacuuming the cars might be followed by a trip to get a bike tune-up and new tires. Reward yourselves as a whole team periodically when you finish a big job. Did you spend half the day spring-cleaning the yard? Celebrate by going out to dinner.

for our children that they were capable of doing or buying for themselves. Our role as parents was and is to help them become independent, productive adults. One way to do this is to create opportunities for children to earn their own money. Encourage them to work and save money for things they dream about.

3. **Honesty.** This is not only the best policy, it is the *only* policy. In addition to being clear about not taking items from friends, neighbors, stores, or family members, we need to teach our kids that even nontangibles—those extra cable channels, time owed our employer, credit for something someone else did—can be stolen. A double standard here is especially dangerous. It's good to ask yourself occasionally, *Is there anything in our home that we should be paying for, but we're not?*

Children will learn a lot about being honest if they see you calling the cable company to report the free service you are receiving, return the extra change when you're given too much, or making every effort to return the item to the rightful owner when you find something that is not yours.

Be sure the consequences for taking something that belongs to someone else is clear. Taking means borrowing something without asking permission, including going in Mom's purse or Dad's wallet to get money for a movie without permission. List the things it means in your family.

4. **Individual worth.** Kids need to understand that they are not what they own, wear, or drive. Each of us is valuable as a unique human being. If the latest fads, fashions, or activities are always a "must" for a child, you have a problem.

This is a sign that the child is seeking identity in material things, not quality of character and personal relationships. It's important that we remind our children regularly of their worth as individuals.

> Be sure your children understand that if they are with a friend who decides to shoplift, the culprit as well as those with him can be charged.

If a child says she wishes she could be like her friend or maybe even belong to that friend's family instead of her own, take the time to listen to what it is she wants that's missing in her life. Perhaps you need to spend more time with her. Perhaps she needs to feel more loved. Perhaps she just needs to hear that every family faces problems and challenges, and usually we can't see those from outside.

The most powerful way we can show our kids that they are valuable is by spending time with them—enjoyable, quality time, and lots of it. Studies show that parents spend an average of just twenty minutes a day communicating with their children, nine of those minutes in disciplinary situations. If you feel you haven't been spending enough positive time with your children, don't get caught in the trap of spending money on them to ease your guilt.

5. **Reality.** Kids need to know that it's a fact of life that none of us always get what we deserve. Sometimes we get more, sometimes less. But most of the time, we will have more than we need. The goal is to be content and thankful for what we have. Talk with your children about how contentment is more a matter of attitude than accumulation. Sometimes younger children understand numbers best. Ask questions such as, "Would you rather have ten toys you didn't want or one toy you really wanted? Why?"

Our kids need to see an attitude of contentment in us. When there is not enough money for what we want, do our children see us griping? Are we content with what we have, or are we always wanting more? It's important that we model what it means to be content, even with the little things of life: a good meal, a comfortable bed, a warm bath, shared family time, or that our day went according to plan.

6. **Generosity.** Even the youngest children can learn to share. When toddlers have the opportunity to play with others, they can begin to understand how to share and be generous.

As kids get older, talk at the dinner table about specific ways you have been treated generously. Brainstorm about how you can live generously. Becoming a family of givers lets your children experience the true satisfaction of giving to someone else. Volunteering as a family in your community can be a fun and memorable way to teach your kids the importance of giving to others. A recent survey revealed that more than a third of American households claim volunteering together as a part of family life. The most popular activities include helping older people, working with youth programs, helping church or religious programs, assisting in sports or school programs, participating in environmental programs, and serving the homeless.

Dollars and Sense

Opportunities to teach kids a healthy respect for money abound. Look for everyday ways to show how actions lead to consequences, and financial ones can be the most rewarding—or the most uncomfortable—of all.

- Let kids be responsible for late charges on videos. Have them start the habit of rewinding rented tapes or putting DVDs in their case immediately after watching and placing them in a designated easy-to-see location near the door. When they forget and you're charged, they can pay.

- Get everyone a library card. Before buying new books, check to see if they're available at the library. When you get home, write the due date on a central family calendar. Put a child in charge of reminding everyone the day to gather books. If someone forgets, let him or her pay the late fee.

- Save money by planning activities that don't cost a lot. For example, learn about an interesting topic or hobby as a family. Research together on the Internet or check out how-to books or videos from the library. Get up early, watch the sun rise, and cook breakfast over a campfire or grill at a park. Go on a bike-hike as a family, ride to a favorite eating spot, then ride back. Call your local parks and recreation department and ask about inexpensive programs and activities that your family might enjoy. Kids can see that fun isn't necessarily expensive.

- Check out local consignment shops before buying furniture or seldom-worn clothing such as ski clothes, formal wear, and boys' blazers. Have kids compare prices so they can see your savings.

- Have your kids fix sack lunches for themselves. You'll save hundreds of dollars a year. Show kids the cost of a typical lunch out—even a fast-food one—and how over weeks and months, that expenditure really drains the bank account.

- Use a debit card instead of credit cards to avoid overspending and accumulating debt. Explain the process to your kids, and tell them why it's important to spend within a budget and avoid debt. Show them some finance charges on loans so they can see how paying over time adds up.

- If possible, go to matinees rather than prime-time, full-price movies. Make sure kids eat before they go. Teach them how expensive concession snacks are by comparing store prices to the ones in the theater.

- Save money by scheduling family haircuts at a beauty or barber school. Have your child call salons to compare prices.

- Take your own rafts and life jackets to water parks or the beach. Renting these items can be expensive, so teach kids by showing them how much money you save by supplying your own equipment.

- Drink water when you eat out at restaurants. This can add up fast if you have a big family. Let kids compute the savings while they're waiting for their meals.

- Take your family's used clothing, books, toys, etc. to a consignment shop. Some will give you more dol-

Swap and Save

- Start a toy-swapping club with other mothers. Trade toys your kids don't mind living without for a couple weeks. The kids will love having different toys often, you'll save money not buying new ones, and the kids will learn the power of bartering.

- Trade lessons with moms with different abilities and gifts from yours. If you enjoy baking, schedule a time to show your child and hers how to bake a great cake. If she's got a green thumb, ask her to have a session with the kids about gardening or plant care.

- Host a neighborhood swap party for videos, costume jewelry, tools, children's or women's clothing, or kitchen utensils. Everyone gets the items she needs without money changing hands.

lars' worth in trade than in cash. Let the kids learn that exchanging is better than throwing away. (One ten-year-old boy I know started his own business selling used books and items on e-Bay.)

- If you can't afford to buy tickets to a special concert or play, find out if you can attend a rehearsal. Show kids that money isn't the only ticket to fun.

- Look into joining your local YMCA or community center instead of a fancy health club; they often provide the same services for a lot less. Compare prices and features, and let your kids see the results.

- Use coupons wisely. Coupons don't save money if they're for products you don't need or that are more expensive than similar products. And if the coupon is for a large-size portion, you might waste most of the food.

    So that kids can learn how to shop for groceries, have them clip coupons and let them keep any money saved. Be sure they check and highlight expiration dates—a good activity to do while watching TV.

- Try no-frills and store brands. Have the kids compare label ingredients and prices. The expensive and generic brands might be identical. If you like them, your small "investment" will pay a high rate of return.

- Have kids know the price of everything you put into your shopping cart and add up what a week's worth of groceries costs.

Everyday Ways to Teach Your Kids Values

Taking care of our children's physical needs is important, but helping them develop strong character is at least as vital. It is our job as parents to shape the character of our children as they grow, to give them a sense of right and wrong, and to provide them with an inner compass that will guide them through life.

None of us will ever be perfect parents, nor will we raise perfect children. But one thing's for sure: If we aim at nothing, we'll probably hit it. Each of us must decide what values and character qualities we want to pass on to our children. Set aside some time, either with your spouse or alone, to make a list of the values you want to pass on to your children. Here are some you might consider. Add your own to the list.

> "Try not to become a man of success but rather try to become a man of value."
> —Albert Einstein

Honesty	Enthusiasm
Kindness	Love of learning
Love	A strong work ethic
Faith	Courage
Patience	Allegiance to country
Self-discipline	Patience
Humility	Care for others
Thanks	Helpfulness
Loyalty	Compassion
Leadership	Respect

The following ideas are simple, everyday ways to build positive character qualities in your child.

- **Be intentional.** Set aside some time to make a list of the values you and your spouse want to pass on to your children.

- **Teach the importance of rules.** When playing board or card games, talk about the importance of playing fairly.

- **Applaud your child at home.** He will be less likely to look desperately for acceptance in the outside world.

- **Talk casually with your child.** For instance, when you run an errand in your car, take your daughter with you. Staring through a windshield can provide a quiet moment to talk about a touchy issue.

- **Be consistent.** Remember that your child is learning even when you're not aware that you're teaching. Don't forget that one day he will follow your example and not your advice.

> "Nobility of character is the most precious heritage of a family, and it is transmitted from generation to generation by personal association and inspiration."
> —Robert McCracken

- **Learn from literature.** Start a collection of good books about teaching values to children.

- **Teach courage.** Be sure your children know that they must stand for something or they'll fall for anything.

If you are the only parent committed to building strong character values into your children, gain strength from Helen Keller's words: "I am only one; but still I am one. I cannot do everything, but still I can do something; I will not refuse to do the something I can do."

- **Expect quality.** Walk out of movies that offend your values, and instruct your kids to do the same.

- **Supervise your kids' intake.** Monitor their television watching and Internet time.

- **Keep the flame alive.** Make your marriage an ongoing priority. It's one of the greatest things you can do for your children.

- **Express your hopes.** Talk with your older children about your dreams for them—that they will live by strong values.

- **Make entertainment educational.** Be alert for television programs and movies that teach values you don't want your children to embrace.

- **Talk about the meaning of this adage:** "You're not necessarily on the right track just because it's a well-beaten path."

- **Build a library.** Start a collection of DVDs or videos and CDs or audio-cassette tapes that entertain your kids and teach them strong values at the same time.

- **Teach consequences.** The decisions we make daily form us into what we will be tomorrow. Small decisions can have a big result—for good or for bad. If your child decides not to do his homework, what are the consequences? Is he happy with his decision? If he decides to do an extra-credit project and gets all sorts of praise from his teacher, again, talk with him about it. Is he glad he decided to do it?

- **Discuss compromise.** Be sure your kids know that if they have to do the wrong thing to stay on the team, they are on the wrong team.

- **Help kids choose their companions.** Be vigilant about your child's friends. For example, if she asks to spend time with someone you know has a high disrespect for authority, let her invite the friend over to your house. If you see that the relationship would not be a healthy one for your child and that your child might not be strong enough to be the leader, talk about this openly.

- **Teach by your own mistakes.** Catch yourself whenever you're inconsiderate or make a mistake. If your child catches you in a lie, acknowledge it and explain that you realize this is wrong. Don't make excuses or try to justify your actions. Admit when you are wrong.

- **Recognize acts of kindness.** Whenever you are with your child and you observe someone being considerate to another, point it out. Always praise your child's acts of kindness.

> *"Nothing makes it easier to resist temptation than a proper bringing up, a sound set of values, and witnesses."*
> —Franklin P. Jones

- **Teach respect for authority.** Daily events offer many occasions for this, but children need to learn it from your example. Do you disregard the law or bad-mouth the school authorities? Remember, more is caught than taught.

- **Honor heroic behavior.** Point out instances in the news and everyday life in which people have been heroic.

- **Teach good manners.** Explain that good manners are a way we show respect for other people (see Teaching Manners, page 115).

- **Offer unseen support.** Pray with and for your children.

Everyday Ways to Teach Children to Be Truthful

- Praise your children for being courageous when they tell the truth even though they know they'll get in trouble.

- Be sure you call a spade a spade and a lie a lie. It's okay to encourage your children's ability to tell imaginative stories. Just be sure you also reinforce the difference between lying and writing or telling a story.

- Half-truths aren't whole. You can make a family "game" of discovering half-truths. Have each person think of an imaginary situation in which he or she might be tempted to tell only half the truth. For example, "I finished my homework—but only after I talked on the phone for an hour with my friend."

■ Don't make promises to your child that you are not willing or able to keep; don't make threats you are not willing to enforce. Your children need to know that telling the truth applies to parents, too.

■ If your child tells a lie, don't take this lightly. Lying was one of the "automatic discipline" behaviors at our house when the boys were growing up.

■ When playing board games or card games with your children, talk about the importance of playing fairly and telling the truth—even when playing a game.

■ When you buy a house or borrow money to buy a car, let your children go with you to the bank. Explain to them the importance of signing a contract—that you are promising, or "telling the truth," that you will fulfill certain obligations.

■ When you catch your child in a lie, be sure she knows that you don't approve of what she did, but you still approve of her.

"He who permits himself to tell a lie once, finds it much easier to do it a second time."
—Thomas Jefferson

■ If your child catches you in a lie, acknowledge it. No excuses. If you are a truthful person, your children will be more likely to be truthful.

■ Never instruct your child to lie for you. If someone you do not want to talk to calls you at home and your child answers the phone, don't ask him to say, "Mom isn't here." If you don't want to accept the call, simply have the child take the caller's number and explain that you will call back later.

■ Do your own truth-in-advertising review. Have family members bring an advertisement clipped from a magazine or newspaper to a family group time. Look at each ad to discover how the truth is being stretched or manipulated. What's the real message of the ad? That we'll be happy, healthy, wise, loved, or pretty if we buy product X?

■ Search out books, videos, and tapes for your child regarding telling the truth. One sure classic is almost any version of "The Boy Who Cried Wolf."

Teaching Good Manners

Good manners do more than make children pleasant to have around; they build confidence in your kids to face varied social situations. As you begin teaching, remember to avoid nagging—be gentle and consistent instead. And don't forget to affirm kids whenever they get it right!

MEALTIME MANNERS
Remind kids to:

- Sit up straight.

- Don't drag your chair across floor or bang silverware against your plate.

- Keep a napkin in your lap, and don't forget to use it.

- Keep chair legs on the floor.

- If the family you're visiting says grace, follow their custom.

- Pass condiments around, not across, the table.

- Don't start eating until everyone has been served.

- Ask the person closest to what you want him or her to "please pass". Thank him or her for doing so.

- Take small portions. Help yourself to seconds after everyone has been served.

- Take what you're offered. If you don't like something, politely say "No, thank you," or take a very small portion.

- Eat slowly. Put down your spoon or fork between bites.

- Chew with your mouth closed.

- Talk only after you've swallowed your food.

- Take small bites.

> "Children have never been very good at listening to their elders, but they have never failed to imitate them." —James Baldwin

Flag Etiquette

Children can be taught at an early age that our flag is special and we treat it with respect. The National Flag Foundation lists some simple rules for honoring our flag:

- You can wear a T-shirt *showing* a flag; do not wear clothes *made of* flags.

- Do not wear pants or use towels bearing flags—the flag should not be sat upon.

- Raise a flag in a lively manner; lower it slowly.

- Don't create a flag motif on a lawn or football field where feet can step on it.

- Don't hang a flag at night unless you can illuminate it.

- Don't display a flag during snow, rain, or other storms unless it is weatherproof.

- Hung vertically, the star-studded section should be in observers' top left corner.

- Swallow food before taking a drink.

- If food is stuck in your teeth, remove it privately after the meal.

- Keep elbows and arms off the table.

- Ask to be excused when the meal is over.

RELATIONSHIP MANNERS

- If your child is rude to you, expect a sincere apology.

- If a disrespectful child visits your home, after he leaves, teach your child about proper manners.

- Practice good introduction manners: Stand and shake hands with adults when meeting them for the first time.

- If you don't hear what someone is saying, say, "Excuse me?" or "Could you respeat what you just said?"

- Make sure your children arrive on time at activities they're invited to—start a lifelong habit! Show them how to call a host if lateness is unavoidable.

- Teach your child to be sensitive to the loner at a party, to invite him or her to participate or to talk.

- When visiting another child's home, instruct your child to offer kitchen help, to keep his belongings organized, and to hang up wet towels.

- Be sure your child says "Thank you" after visiting someone.

- If the visit was special in some way, or lasted longer than a night, work with your child on a thank you note to mail the hosts.

THANK YOU NOTES

- Express thanks as soon as you can.

- Whenever possible, write your gratitude in a note. The receiver will savor reading this tangible expression.

- Mention the specific gift you received and any special features you appreciate.

- Don't be flowery; be sincere.

- Encourage your kids to start this habit early. Here's a sample note for kids to follow:

Date
Dear (name),

   Thank you for all the fun things you did for me when I came to visit you. I especially enjoyed (list something you really liked doing). *Thank you for* (name something that was done for you, such as a special bed made for you or a food or treat you liked). *I hope to see you again very soon.*

   Love, (Sincerely yours, or Your friend,)

   (name)

Raising a Spiritual Child

Home is the spiritual forming ground for the mortals in your midst. It is here that we initiate the moral standard-bearing, the spiritual hunger, the legacy of love that we hope our children will choose to emulate.

Faith is important for everyone. Like all worthy pursuits, it can and should be kid-friendly—accessible, interesting, something they can develop at their own speed. Here are some tips for putting lifelong faith within a child's reach:

> **"The virtues of mothers shall be visited upon their children."**
> —**Charles Dickens**

- Become comfortable with your own faith. All of us need a way to answer the deep questions of life: Where did I come from? Why am I here? Where am I going? Does life have any meaning or purpose? Talk about other religions with your children and compare them with your own beliefs.

- Create an atmosphere in which your kids can openly ask questions and work through their beliefs. Honest wonderings, and even honest doubts, deserve straightforward discussion and answers.

- Sit near the front of your place of worship so your children can see what's happening and feel more involved in the worship service.

- Sing hymns or songs from your faith as you put your child to bed at night.

- Buy a children's version of the Bible for your child.

- Help your child get involved in a church youth group or Bible study. Peers with like values can encourage each other to live up to high standards.

- Remind older children getting ready to go off to college that their beliefs about God may be questioned and even ridiculed. Be sure they are grounded in what is true and are ready to defend their faith.

- As a family, start your day at the breakfast table reminding your children of God's presence. Every morning before school at our house, we read a chapter from the Book of Proverbs, which teaches wise living, then said a prayer for our day.

- See to it that your own spiritual life is growing so you can be a source of strength and wisdom for your children.

- Begin a prayer journal for your children. Date your prayers and what you pray for.

Teaching Life Skills

It's never too early to begin teaching your kids important life skills. To make the learning process enjoyable, remember to be patient. Be prepared for your children to struggle at first, and encourage every step of their progress until they learn.

CHILDREN AGES 5–8 CAN LEARN HOW TO:

- Set the table.

- Sweep.

- Make a bed.

- Help with laundry: fold flat items, match socks, and put things away.

- Pick up clutter.

- Answer the telephone politely.

- Load the dishwasher with unbreakables.

- Cook something simple with supervision such as a grilled cheese sandwich or French toast.

- Wash off a wound and get a Band-Aid.

- Identify poisonous plants.

- Dial 911 for help.

- Respond if confronted by a stranger.

CHILDREN AGES 9–12 CAN LEARN HOW TO:

- Sew on buttons and do simple mending.

- Use a washer and dryer and decide which product to use—stain remover, detergent, bleach, softener—and when.

- Iron simple items with supervision.

- Operate kitchen appliances.

- Safely use a knife.

- Administer basic first aid.

- Use different kinds of household cleaners.

- Write and follow a simple budget.

- Hammer and remove nails.

- Use a screwdriver.

- Read a road map.

- Put air in tires.

- Wash a car.

- Wrap gifts.

TEENAGERS CAN LEARN HOW TO:

- Plan and cook meals.

- Do business at a bank—open an account, balance a checkbook, and make deposits and withdrawals.

- Set up appointments over the telephone.

- Write a résumé and interview for a job.

- Iron clothes.

- Fix a leaky faucet.

- Mow the lawn.

- Change a flat tire.

- Jump-start a car.

- Pump gasoline.

- Check oil level and tire pressure on car.

- Perform CPR.

- Unstop a toilet.

Pets as Teachers

Letting children have a pet is a great way to teach them responsibility, and if you breed the pet, it's a natural way to teach sex education. To make an informed decision about bringing a pet into your home, consider the needs and demands each pet might have. Here's fodder for your decision.

Dogs usually live ten years or more and require:

- A bed or outdoor housing.

- Feeding once per day.

- Fresh water daily.

- At least one hour of grooming daily. Long coats need daily brushing, short coats, weekly.

- Baths at least every three months.

- Lots of attention. Dogs love company and need to play several hours a day, inside and out.

- Vet visits once upon purchase, then twice a year. Additional visits for neutering or spaying and worm treatment might be necessary.

- A medium amount of expense.

> "I am fond of pigs. Dogs look up to us. Cats look down on us. Pigs treat us as equal."
> —Winston Churchill

SELECTING A PUPPY

- Buy from a family or breeder where you know the dog has been properly treated. The doggie in the window at the pet store might be cute, but they have often been raised someplace where they were not properly treated.

- Getting a dog at an animal shelter might be socially responsible, but be wise. You don't know what kind of environment the dog was raised in, so determine the dog's temperament. Avoid big breeds that could be dangerous, and spend plenty of time with the dog before you take it home.

- If possible, see the puppy's parents. Like children, puppies often grow up with temperaments similar to their parents.

- The best time to get a puppy is when it is six to nine weeks old. Puppies that remain with their litter longer than sixty-three days can develop personality problems.

- The puppy that comes to you is not always the best one to pick. Caution with a stranger is often a sign of intelligence.

Cats usually live ten years or more and require:

- A quiet indoor bed.

- Feeding twice per day.

- Fresh water daily.

- Grooming for half an hour per day. Long coats need daily brushing; short coats, twice weekly.

- A medium amount of attention.

- Two vet visits as a kitten, then annual visits plus any trips for worms, neutering, or spraying.

- A medium amount of expense.

Birds live from five to sixty-plus years, depending on breed, and require:

- A cage or perch or if they live outdoors a mesh-covered aviary.

- Feeding once per day.

- Fresh water daily.

- Twenty minutes of care per day (more if you're training a bird to talk).

- A medium amount of attention.

Selecting a Kitten

Healthy kittens will have clean and dry ears, a pink mouth with white teeth, a smooth coat, and a damp nose. They should be lively and inquisitive.

- A long-term commitment. Parakeets live six years; canaries, five to ten; parrots, sixty or more.

- Vet visits when sick, and possibly trips for beak and nail trimming.

- A small amount of expense.

Fish live from two to ten years and require:

- An aquarium or large bowl; outdoor pond for goldfish if desired.

- Feeding once or twice per day.

- Clean, aerated water to swim in.

- aquarium or bowl cleaned once a month.

- A small amount of attention.

- Vet care only when ill.

- A small to medium amount of expense.

Horses and *ponies* live from twenty to thirty-five years and require:

- Fenced pasture or paddock; a barn or stable.

- Food and water twice per day at regular intervals.

- At least thirty minutes per day of grooming, cleaning, and exercising.

- Horseshoe maintenance and replacement.

- Lots of attention: frequent riding and hoof cleaning and daily grooming.

- Vet care twice a year.

- A large amount of expense.

Rats and *mice* live from three to four years and require:

- A cage.

- Constantly available food and water.

- Cage cleaning daily for mice; weekly for rats.

- A medium amount of attention.

- Vet care if sick.

- A small amount of expense.

Gerbils live from one to five years and require:

- A cage.

- Constantly available food and water.

- Cage cleaning weekly.

- A medium amount of attention. Hold pet every day to maintain tameness.

- Vet care when sick.

- A small amount of expense.

Hamsters live from one to four years and require:

- A cage.

- Constantly available food and water.

- Cage cleaning weekly.

- A small amount of attention. Cage alone, and hold frequently to maintain tameness.

- Vet care when sick.

- A small amount of expense.

Rabbits live from five to ten years and require:

- Indoor cage or weatherproof shelter outside.

- Feeding once per day with food pellets as well as grass cuttings and hay.

- Fresh water daily.

- Cage cleaning weekly.

- Grooming weekly for short-haired; daily for long-haired.

- A large amount of attention: lots of holding and petting. Cage females together.

- Vet care when sick.

- A small amount of expense.

Guinea pigs live from four to five years and require:

- A cage.

- Daily feeding with pellets and hay.

- Fresh water daily.

- Cage cleaning daily.

- Frequent brushing if long-haired.

- A medium amount of attention.

- Vet care when sick.

- A small amount of expense.

Safety Essentials for an Unsafe World

Teach young children to recite their names, address, and phone number. If basic memorization is difficult for them, try singing the information to a familiar tune. Learn the new song together.

- Help your children understand that they should never get in a car with anyone but their parents or other close relatives.

- Develop a special code word that can be used if someone else must pick up your children. Teach your children to ask for that word before getting in a car, even with someone familiar.

- List those friends and neighbors with whom your children are allowed to visit or ride.

- Show your children how, if they get lost or need help, to dial 911 from your home phone and a pay phone. Explain that they don't need change to use this number at a public phone.

- Teach your children never to go into a public bathroom alone.

- Explain to your children when they are allowed to say no to adults.

- Have your children practice being loud if they feel threatened by a stranger.

- Teach your children to protect themselves physically if they find themselves in dangerous situations.

- Help your children understand that they should never leave a mall, store, or other public place with a stranger, no matter what he or she says.

- Practice how to ask a policeman or other uniformed personnel for help if they need it.

- Teach your children what body parts are not okay for others to touch.

- Train your children to shout "Stop!" or "No!" if someone touches them in an off-limits place.

- Tell your children that you will love them no matter what happens.

- Teach your children how to respond if someone they trust asks them to do something they know is wrong or about which they feel uncomfortable.

- *Never leave your children alone in your car or in a public setting.*

■ Know your children's friends and their families. Be sure you have their addresses and phone numbers.

■ Know what path your children take to travel to and from school.

Discuss and practice how children should handle the following:

■ Answering the phone and taking messages.

■ Visiting a friend's house or having a friend visit.

■ Losing the house key.

■ Staying after school.

■ Missing the bus or car pool.

■ Accidental injury, choking, or poisoning.

■ Weather emergencies or fire.

■ A stranger makes threats, hassles, or sexual advances.

■ A stranger on the phone or at the front door.

■ A stranger asks for his or her name.

Internet Safety

As responsible parents, we would never knowingly allow our children to communicate with a deviant. Yet if we allow our children unsupervised access to the Internet, we run the risk of this very thing happening. Here's how you can protect your kids:

■ Become more computer literate. Get to know the services your child uses. Find out what types of information they offer and whether there are built-in ways to block out objectionable material.

■ Consider using a pseudonym or "unlisting" your child's name if your service allows it. Steer away from online profiles. Pedophiles often use profiles as a means to find victims.

■ Never allow a child to arrange a face-to-face meeting with another computer user without permission. If a meeting is arranged, make the first meeting in a public place and accompany your child to the meeting.

■ Do not allow your child to respond to messages or bulletin board items that are suggestive, obscene, belligerent, or threatening. Forward a copy of such messages to your Internet service provider.

■ Call the National Center for Missing and Exploited Children at 1-800-843-5678 if you are aware of the transmission, use, or viewing of child pornography online.

■ Never give out any personal information such as your address, telephone number, work number, or your child's school name.

■ Keep the computer in your family room where you can watch and monitor your child's activities.

■ Share an e-mail account with your child so you can oversee his or her mail.

■ Spend as much time as possible online together to show your children proper behavior and rules.

■ Do not allow your children to go into private chat rooms without your being present.

■ Monitor your credit card bill. Many pornographic Internet sites require credit card payments to gain access. Consider using an online service that has special child accounts with restricted access to chat rooms and the Internet.

■ Always keep in mind that as you move through the Internet, you leave information about yourself. When a user posts to USENET.IRC chat rooms or listservers, the user reveals his mailing address so others can contact him. Some websites also collect information called "cookies." Cookies are compiled lists of information that might include your name, address, telephone number, and possibly even your credit card number. Ask your Internet service provider how to turn off your cookies.

Making Peace with Your Teenager

When people hear the word *leadership,* they think of presidents, CEOs, head coaches, and the like. But a person doesn't need a fancy title or an oval office to be a powerful leader. In fact, mothers are perhaps the strongest informal leaders in the world. We are shaping the next generation.

Although teens think they are smarter than their parents, they're not. They don't have the experience and wisdom to make all their own decisions or to face life's problems alone. They still need discipline and love. And most of all, they need to be encouraged, under your courageous mother-leadership, to begin to think and behave responsibly on an adult level.

> "There is no influence so powerful as that of the mother."
> —Sarah Joseph Hall

When my kids entered the teenage years, in my own quest to be a good mother-leader—a powerful influence for good over the teens for whom I am responsible—I read a lot of books on the topic and interviewed many different types of leaders. I learned ten characteristics of effective leadership and applied them to being the mother of teenagers.

1. **Leaders have a strong sense of purpose.** They know where they are going. They stand for something. They are not easily blown off-course. They know what they want to achieve and focus their energy on getting there.

In this day of anything-goes values, teenagers need to know their family's purpose or vision—and that it is firmly fixed. They need constants that serve as anchors for them in the turbulent sea of adolescence.

Does your teen know your family's standards and values? In our family, we decided corporately that our family purpose would be to create an atmosphere in our home where each family member might be nurtured and encouraged to become all he or she was created to be, so that we might make an impact on our culture—individually and corporately—in a positive way.

2. **Leaders are persistent.** They are willing to put in the time and effort required to reach their goal. Persistence separates the leader from the dreamer.

Let's face it, motherhood is hard work. It demands patience, sacrifice, tenacity, long hours at low pay, resilience under fire, and sometimes we have to be bulldog-stubborn. Like Winston Churchill said, "The nose of a bulldog has been slanted backward so that it can breathe without letting go."

There are many times we are called on to do the same. We have to be bulldog-stubborn when we see our teens act irresponsibly. We have to take a strong (and typically unpopular) stand against blatantly immoral movies and television programs *everyone else's* mom allows. Sometimes we must turn off the radio and talk about the questionable lyrics of a song *everyone else* thinks is okay. We have to say no to chat rooms *everyone else* thinks are harmless. And sometimes our stubborn commitment is displayed in our refusal to give up on a child—continuing to love the child although we hate his behavior.

3. **Leaders take risks.** Leaders take calculated gambles with people, money, and ideas. The prospects of not trying are more onerous than not succeeding.

Mothers take risks every day. We let our children ride their bikes to the park or drive a car to school during morning rush-hour traffic. Every time they're out on dates, it's a risk. But we have to let them grow up. Children need to experience freedom gradually while we are close by to help. Every time we let out the rope, we take a risk. They could fall. They could abuse their new freedom. But we are close enough to monitor their progress and catch them before they fall too hard.

4. **Leaders are able to attract and energize people.** They are like magnets. They ignite, inspire, and draw people around a common effort or goal. What draws people to a leader? An attitude of servanthood. People want to follow someone who they know has their best interests at heart.

It might sound redundant to call upon mothers to adopt an attitude of servanthood. It's almost part of the definition of motherhood. But unfortunately, I know women who think of their children as a bother or an imposition they can't wait to get rid of. These women produce double misery. After all, what teenager would want to follow a leader who can't wait until he's gone?

Lamentably, I also meet women who are so insecure they are living their lives through their children. On the surface they look like adoring mothers, but come the teen years, when children begin to assert their independence, the truth becomes clear. The mothers are using their children to build their own self-esteem. Kids know this instinctively and find another leader they think they can trust.

5. Leaders believe in their followers. They are able to establish relationships based on trust, respect, and care. They accept people as they are, don't dwell on past mistakes, and radiate confidence in their followers' future.

Anyone who accepts the position of motherhood had best be ready to dish out forgiveness or else live in the garbage heap of her own hurt emotions. Teenagers need to be confronted with their irresponsible behavior, but they need heavy doses of forgiveness and unconditional love when they fail. They need to know we trust and have confidence in them even when they don't please us—and even when it's hard to trust them. Leaders know that the best way to make someone trustworthy is to trust him—and the surest way to make him untrustworthy is to distrust him and show their mistrust.

6. Leaders know their strengths and limitations. They don't try to do everything. They know what they do well and stick to it.

When it comes to motherhood, like you, I wear a lot of hats—some of which don't fit very well. But a few do fit well, and these are the things I focus on.

If you've read my other books, you know that many of my meals should be served with a side dish of antacids. The kitchen is not my power alley, and because of this, I spent many years feeling as if I were an inferior mother. Then I realized that there's no such thing as a perfect mother. All of us have strong suits and weak suits, and if we're smart managers, we'll try to do more of what we do best and, whenever possible, let someone else do what we're not good at.

If you're not a good cook, don't let that stop you from hosting midnight breakfasts after prom. Fix easy dishes, or better still, delegate food to another mom. You take care of decorations or organizing activities or taking photos the kids will cherish forever.

7. Leaders are learners. They consider themselves students, not experts who know it all. They can learn from anyone with something to teach them.

It is important for our teenagers that we set the model of teachability. If we come across as having arrived, not only do we miss the opportunity to learn ourselves, but we set an example our teens will follow when we want to teach them something.

I learned an important lesson from man who told the story of passing by the window of one of his college professors every morning at 5:30 A.M. on his way to work, then again at 11 P.M. on his way back home. The professor was always sitting at this window, studying. Finally the man asked the professor why he kept studying. After all, he was the teacher. He should have already known everything. The professor answered, "Son, I would rather have my students drink from a running stream than a stagnant pool."

This story made a great impression on me as a mother. I decided to never stop learning so I might set an example for my children, be able to understand what my children were studying, and stimulate their learning process at home.

The day we put our brains on the shelf and stop learning about motherhood—and other subjects as well—is the day we stifle significant communication with our teenagers. Here's a good philosophy to live by and pass on to our kids: As long as we live, we learn; and as long as we learn, we live.

8. **Leaders are passionate and positive about their work.** They have a contagious enthusiasm about what they do.

It bears repeating: Motherhood is an incredible privilege. Sure, there are probably plenty of days when you want to throw up your hands and scream when you find the pantry empty again, for the fourth time in a week, because the kids and their friends want to hang out at your house. And you might wonder how much longer you can tolerate your daughter's favorite band, who, in her opinion, has the potential to make it to the top. (Maybe you wonder, *The top of what?*)

There are difficult seasons in every mother's life. No one is without problems. But leaders are committed to working through and learning from hardships. They look for something good in even the worst of circumstances. Yes, the pantry's empty, but you're thankful you know what the kids are up to because they're hanging out at your house. The music is unpleasant, but at least the lyrics are not derogatory. As a mom, be committed to looking for the good in everything.

9. **Leaders are self-disciplined.** They don't indulge their fears or their appetites. They take care of the inner part of their lives. The result is integrity. What they say and do is what they are.

What this means in my role as a mother is this: If I ask my children to take care of their bodies, to censor what goes into their minds, to nourish their spirits, and to strive for excellence in their studies, I do the same. I must model the behaviors I want them to embrace.

10. Leaders don't dwell on mistakes or blame others for their problems. They don't wallow in their failure; they admit when they are wrong and own up to their part of a problem.

If you're the mother of a teenager and things are not going as well in your relationship as you'd hoped, don't blame yourself and say, "If only I had done this. If only I had done that. . . ." Instead, focus your energies in a more positive way. Instead of saying, "If only," try asking, "What now?" It's never too late mend fences and make changes. Perhaps you need to sit down with a child and ask forgiveness for your part in a relational rift—even if you think you're only 5 percent of the problem. As the mother-leader, admit your mistakes, confirm your love, and confess you're committed to learning how to be a better mom. Your willingness to listen and learn will go a long way.

THE TEENAGER-PARENT CONTRACT

It's important for parents to talk to teenagers about behavioral guidelines and expectations as well as the consequences of not adhering to the standards you and your

> *"If discipline were practiced in every home, juvenile delinquency would be reduced by 95 percent."* —J. Edgar Hoover

spouse agree upon. Be specific about what is and isn't acceptable behavior. A good way to do this is with a contract between you and your son or daughter. You and your child should sign and date the contract so that if an infringement occurs, they won't be able to use "I didn't know I wasn't supposed to do that" as an excuse.

(Visit www.familymanager.com to download and print a Parent-Teenager Contract.)

Here are some sample points you might include in your contract.

- My opinion matters a lot, but this is not a democracy, so my parents have the final say.

- I will express my freedom responsibly. I will ask permission when I'm not sure what my parents would want me to do.

- Every member of my family is valuable, so I will treat each person and any guest in my home with respect and thoughtfulness.

- I will also not abuse family members physically or verbally—including rudeness, swearing, or name-calling.

- I will treat my body and anyone else's with deep respect. No drugs or cigarettes are allowed. No pornography or sexual contact between unmarried persons is allowed. I will not consume any alcohol without my parents' consent.

- Unless I have previously discussed an exception, I will be home by _____ on weeknights and _____ on Friday and Saturday nights and always let Mom or Dad know where I am at all times.

- I agree to be truthful in all things.

- I understand that having belongings is a privilege, not a right, so I will take care of my possessions and respect other's property as well. I will ask before borrowing, knock before entering, and treat someone else's possessions as I would my own.

- I will exercise responsibility with my time. Responsibilities come before privileges, so I will get homework and chores done before television, computer time, or goofing-off time.

Helping a Teenager Grow in Responsibility and Integrity

As our children enter the teenage years, we hope they have internalized the code of ethics we have been teaching them and drawn their moral boundaries. Whether you feel their standards are firmly anchored or still a little fuzzy, it's a good idea to talk about this important issue. Make it a priority to schedule some time to ask your children to describe the personal guidelines they feel they should set for themselves as they begin to go out on their own more frequently without your supervision. If they don't know how to verbalize their answers, you can help them out by presenting some scenarios in which they could likely find themselves faced with hard decisions. For example, ask how he or she would respond in the following situations:

"Those who would be free must be virtuous." —Clinton Rossiter

- You learn that a friend is using or selling drugs.

- You find out that many students at your school think it's no big deal to cheat on tests.

- You learn a simple way to sneak in and out of a friend's house.

- You are asked to do something "just for fun" you know is against the law.

- You are at a party that's getting out of hand. Kids are drinking, and you begin to question the safety of the people at the party, including yourself.

- You are offered the opportunity to make money doing something that goes against your conscience.

- You have the opportunity to get a false ID.

- A friend confides that she was date raped.

- A friend starts talking about suicide.

When your growing child faces a tough choice, the fact that he's thought through the situation beforehand doesn't guarantee a better response, but it will make it easier for him to make a wise decision. And remember, you know your child better than anyone else—sometimes even better than he knows himself. Every human being has blind spots—the black holes of life we get sucked into because of our personality, natural tendencies, or upbringing. Maybe you've never thought about it in this way, but you've probably noticed some of your child's black-hole tendencies from a very young age.

Have you ever said something like, "My daughter's known how to get her way since she was three years old" or "My son has tried to bend the rules since day one"? As innocent as these tendencies might seem, they are potential black holes. By helping your child anticipate some of the challenges he might face, you can help him develop the wisdom and self-discipline to step away when tempted to do things that don't reflect his values.

> "'Tis easier to prevent bad habits than to break them."
> —Benjamin Franklin

Helping Teenagers Make Peace with Their Changing Bodies

When a child hits adolescence, both the teen and the mom are in for an adventure. Your son's or daughter's body is changing drastically, and you both must get used to new height, weight, appetite, and appearance. And with your teen's body producing more oil and odor than ever before, you need to help your child develop healthy hygiene habits.

This is about more than smelly armpits or zits. When teens learn to make themselves presentable, they up their confidence, feel more relaxed with who they are, and can relate more openly with the people around them.

It's not necessarily a smooth road—for you or your child. Your teen needs to learn, without being defensive, that he must make more effort at hygiene than ever before. Your job is to encourage this behavior without nagging.

It can be a tricky time, because many mothers lack confidence when talking with kids, particularly boys, about grooming and hygiene. They sense their child's embarrassment, or they project their own. And teens might have questions they're too shy to ask or secretly feel hurt when Mom keeps suggesting, "Take a shower" or "Don't forget to put on deodorant."

The key here is to respect your teen's new need for privacy and independence and approach him sensitively. Here are some tips to help you steer clear of awkward conversations or harping too much on the hygiene habit. Remember, the goal is to teach your teen good grooming because in doing so, you are grooming him for life.

- Leave helpful information to read about good grooming and hygiene on teens' dressers. In front of you they may feign disinterest, but deep down, they care.

- Purchase appealing grooming products and leave them in the bathroom for teens to try. For years, girls have had fruity, flowery options from which to choose, but guys have either had to smell like their sister or borrow Dad's "old-man" products, which, according to my boys, is not a great option. Finally, product manufacturers have wised up and realized that boys want their own grooming products. I wish OT, a new line of personal grooming products for boys, had been around when my guys realized that smelling like a locker room is not a good thing.

- Keep on hand a supply of clean underwear and socks—the kinds they like. Although teenagers should be doing their own laundry, you can score big Mom Points if you have a secret stash for the times they get behind and need to be rescued.

- Explain how, when, and why various products are used in short, casual conversations while in the store or when the right circumstances arise. Few boys know the difference between a deodorant and antiperspirant without being told. Girls know more about hygiene products but might be bashful about discussing the use of things like tampons. Helpful, factual conversations help build trust.

- Be aware of teens' need to feel good about themselves. Adjust your schedule, and encourage them to set their alarms, to allow them enough time in the bathroom each morning. Buy your teenage daughter a makeup mirror. Even if she doesn't like to wear makeup, she probably needs to tweeze her brows. Let a professional cosmetologist show your daughter how to lightly apply makeup to bring out her natural beauty.

- Be sensitive to their preoccupation with appearance and self-image. Avoid teasing them or joking at their expense. Words are powerful and can hurt as much as they can help. A casual put-down, even made humorously, is just that: a put-down. It lingers in a teen's mind and chips away at his or her self-esteem.

- Be sure your teenagers have places at home that give them a sense of ownership and privacy. They need some time and space that allows them to reflect, spend time alone, try on clothes, practice shaving (faces or legs), and chill out after a demanding day at school. If they share a room with a sibling, work out a plan for some alone time in the room.

- Help your maturing children achieve a healthy balance in their lives. Besides school and extracurricular activities, be sure they get plenty of rest, practice good eating habits, get daily exercise, receive spiritual input and guidance, and have time for fun and laughter. All these contribute to their feelings of well-being and self-assurance.

- Show unconditional love in tangible ways. As adolescents' bodies are growing up and out, their emotions are running rampant: Guys are trying to understand who they are and how they fit into the world. Girls are wondering if they're pretty enough—whether they're pretty at all—and how their girlfriends will view their fashion choices. Both wonder how to deal with the opposite sex and whether everything they feel and think is normal. Although adolescents can be cruel in criticizing the appearances of their peers, often teens are their own harshest critics. In a world where performance means everything, kids need to know that at home, the tryouts are over. They are always "good enough."

- Remember that you're promoting good hygiene for a variety of reasons: to improve appearance and maintain health; to help them cope with dramatically different bodies; and to arm them for deflecting negative comments, teasing, or criticisms just by being sure they won't reek after gym or get a greasy-hair jab in homeroom.

- Be sensitive to the fact that adolescents are more concerned about their appearance than they let on—surveys prove it. That disheveled look so popular these days is carefully coifed, gelled, and pasted into well-planned place. Teens strive for that delicate balance of being noticed but not being noticed too much. Be generous with compliments.

- Conscientious hygiene does more than make teenagers look and smell better; it makes them *feel* better, and this actually improves their performance in school. Experts say that kids can be so preoccupied with how they smell or whether their hair looks weird that they can't listen attentively in class. Feeling at ease with their bodies gives teenagers the peace of mind to pay closer attention in class.

- Learn to ask specific questions. Teens are notoriously noncommunicative. Ask questions that encourage dialogue. Instead of asking, "How was your day?" ask "Do you need particular school supplies for classes or products for showering after gym?"

Teens have a natural, healthy need for independence. Growing into responsible adults is a good thing! But their instinctual need to assert independence often supercedes even the best advice. Don't nag or even strongly advocate on matters of hygiene and grooming without expecting a push back. Present the facts, offer the products, think creatively, and remind your teenage son or daughter of your unflinching love.

> ### Smart Move
>
> Visit www.kidshealth.org for helpful information from medical experts for parents, kids, and teens.

More Practical Ways to Be a Good Mom to a Teenager

- Create a warm and welcoming atmosphere in your home so your teenagers and their friends will want to hang out there. They'll have a safe, fun place to go, and you'll know what they're doing. Keep plenty of soda and snacks on hand, and be willing to put up with some mess and some louder-than-pleasant music.

- Take a look at yourself from your teenagers' perspective. Do they look up to you as the type of adult they want to be someday?

- Create opportunities for your teenagers to be around kids a few years older who can serve as role models. Adopt a college student attending school in your area. Invite him or her over for weekend meals and to share family holidays.

- Send your child to a good summer camp. It helps tremendously for kids to not only learn how to make wise decisions from their parents, but also from older peers they look up to. At camp, kids can learn flexibility, independence, and responsibility. They can also enhance their athletic and social skills, develop self-discipline, and grow in character. Ask a church or synagogue in your area for suggestions of good camps in your area, or visit www.cciusa.org for a list of camps by region.

- Where are you leading your family? Carve an evening out of your schedule and discuss your family's vision and purpose. Vision is a clear mental image of a desired future state. Discuss your teenagers' strengths and abilities, and help them dream grand dreams about what they can achieve. Have each family member write a personal vision statement, and corporately write a vision statement for your family.

- Don't bury your head in the sand. Listen to your children's music. Especially find out what they're listening to via headphones. Question the lyrics. When I had teenagers, I enrolled in an exercise class that played popular music, not only for the exercise, but to keep up with what my kids were hearing on the radio. Ask your kids if they understand the lyrics of their favorite songs. Research shows that when our minds receive an image six times, it becomes indelibly etched there. Don't foolishly think that lyrics with messages about casual sex, rebellion, and suicide are not affecting your child's decisions.

> "My mother was the source from which I derived the guiding principles of my life."
> —John Wesley

- Help your kids network with other kids who have like values and ambitions. Before our boys started high school, we hosted a party for kids they had met from other schools who would soon be attending the same high school. We regularly hosted get-togethers all through their high-school years.

- Let your teenagers know you're on their team. Show an interest in their friends, schoolwork, and activities without being pushy or judgmental.

- Stand up for right and wrong. Set limits on what they see on television and at the movies as long as they live in your home. Just because they may be able to walk into an R-rated movie doesn't mean you have to condone watching immoral or violent behavior in your family room.

- Think of creative ways to show your teenagers your love. One mom I know becomes the Finals Fairy to relieve the pressure when her daughter is studying for final exams. She buys her small gifts and writes humorous poems.

When one of our boys wanted to pursue a friendship with a boy we knew was headed for trouble, we took the opportunity to talk about the importance of choosing good friends and the effect they have on our lives. During this time, my husband and I planned plenty of teenager-friendly activities and weekend family trips so when we said no to some things, we were able to offer and say yes to other fun things.

- Show your teens you care by treating their schoolwork and desks as you would your own business. Be sure they have plenty of supplies, good lighting, and a pleasant atmosphere in their "offices" (see Homework Hints for Success, page 95). Work with teens to establish some guidelines about whether music can be played, snacks can be eaten, etc. while they are studying.

- Help your teenagers give a graduation or going-away party for a friend. This says you care about what's important to them.

- Put together photo albums for your children with pictures of them over the years. Present these at graduation.

- Buy your teens books on subjects they love or CDs or tapes of their favorite artists. Present these to them out of the blue with a note saying, "Thanks for being such a terrific kid."

- Help your teenagers start a business or get a job. Brainstorm about their talents and resources, then think of a need they could meet. Help them write a good résumé. Teach them the importance of looking people in the eye and shaking hands firmly when being interviewed.

- Think of ways to show your children you care about their worlds. Clip magazine and newspaper articles pertaining to subjects they are studying in school. File them by category for easy retrieval when needed.

Sex Education: A Parent's Responsibility

Messages about sex are everywhere, and one thing's for sure: If we don't talk to our children about sex, they will get the information on their own from the media or their peers—and it could be faulty, even harmful, information. It is parents' responsibility to give kids accurate, practical information. I'm not talking about scheduling one night to have a big-deal sex education talk with your child with hopes that he'll listen. This is not a "Whew, I got that out of the way" issue.

Here are ideas for passing on a healthy view of sex to your children:

- Be positive and honest. Tell your children what you believe is right and wrong about sex. Realize that your teens will probably not listen to your opinions if you seem to be judging their friends or teachers. Know the facts and present them in love. Remind them of your lifetime commitment to their health, security, and well-being.

- Be a role model. Practice what you preach. If you tell your children to live one way but you clearly behave in another way, the message they will get is that you don't really believe what you're telling them is important.

- Be accessible and approachable. What they ask may shock you at times, but just be thankful that they're asking and willing to talk to you.

- Make good information available. Have appropriate books, videos, and pamphlets around the house for your children to use when they want to. Remember, the less you push, the more likely they are to take a look. Research the Internet for contact information for the Physicians Resource Council in your state. They offer free resources and literature. Or ask your pastor or rabbi for suggestions.

- Ask questions. What are your children learning in school? It might surprise you, and it will also give you a chance to add some of your own values and opinions. Allow your children to have an opinion. Listening is a good way to get your children to open up.

- Remember that sex is good and hormones are real. Curiosity about sex will not go away just because you never discuss the subject. In fact, avoiding the subject can make sex seem even more exciting. Reinforce your values. Talk about what you believe. Avoid leaving a lot of gray areas. Tell your children you are proud when they make mature, healthy decisions.

- Trust them. Tell your children that you intend to trust them. Praise them when they earn that trust. When they make mistakes (and they will), talk about how they can correct these mistakes and win back your trust. Don't leave them feeling hopeless.

Preparing Your Child for College

Here it is: the first almost-adult choice your teenager has to make. And it's a big one. Be sure to help all you can without forcing your choice on your son or daughter. The search should begin at least eighteen months in advance, and it shouldn't be influenced by your own fond memories of the old alma mater.

- Along with your teen, research potential choices. Talk honestly about tuition and other expenses. Encourage your teen to share goals, concerns, and expectations.

- Visit as many schools as you can. Check to see if a college will be in session, and plan a meeting with someone from the admissions office. If the whole family can't attend, trade off visits with your spouse.

- During senior year, your teen will need to begin narrowing his choices. Help him or her create a compare-and-contrast sheet to see how different schools measure up. Rate each in the following categories from one to five, with five being the highest:

  Annual tuition
  Living costs
  Availability of financial aid
  Availability of proposed major
  Other academic strengths
  Other benefits (good music department, strong sports team, etc.)
  Distance from home
  Overall rank

- Be prepared to fill out parts of college applications and financial aid applications, and keep your tax records handy.

DEPARTURE DAY COUNTDOWN

10. You and your spouse should each spend some private time with your teen. Don't forget to remind your departing teen of the risky behavior that happens on college campuses. Ask him or her to consider your family's values when faced with difficult choices.

Send your college student a final-exams survival kit. Include a mug and instant cocoa mix a tin of homemade cookies, energy bars, pens and pencils, highlighters, and a note that says "I love you!"

9. If your teen wants a going-away party, help put it together.

8. Shop together for necessities. Don't buy too many clothes; leave some money in the teen's budget so he or she can purchase the "in" items at school.

7. Two weeks before departure, start packing. If your child will be traveling by airplane, ship boxes a week ahead or, if you're traveling with him or her, purchase some items at your destination.

6. Plan a special family dinner for the college-bound teen. Consider putting together a *This Is Your Life* video program or displaying photos of the honoree's childhood in the kitchen or family room. Involve your other kids in these opportunities to toast, or roast, their sibling.

5. Even if you plan to keep your teen's room as is, with your teen's input go through his or her files and bookcases, putting away school mementos. Sort clothing into piles to be packed, to be left at home, and to be given away.

4. Provide your teen with a credit card, carefully explaining what purchases are okay to use it on.

3. Create a family album. Slip it into the teen's luggage or present it when you arrive at the school.

2. Remind your college teen that you love him or her.

1. Make plans to keep in touch by phone—a prepaid phone card or a home 800 number is a good investment.

College Checklist

ROOM SUPPLIES

- [ ] Backpack
- [ ] Travel kit
- [ ] Tote bag
- [ ] Lamp
- [ ] Framed photo of family
- [ ] Fan
- [ ] Trash can
- [ ] Extension cord
- [ ] Write-on memo board
- [ ] Bulletin board
- [ ] Posters
- [ ] Alarm clock or clock radio
- [ ] Stereo
- [ ] CDs
- [ ] CD holder
- [ ] Over-the-door hooks
- [ ] Trunk
- [ ] Hangers
- [ ] Double-up rod
- [ ] Stacking baskets
- [ ] Milk crates
- [ ] Luggage ID tags
- [ ] Under-bed storage boxes
- [ ] Jewelry box
- [ ] Adhesive hooks
- [ ] Throw rug
- [ ] Scrapbook
- [ ] Reclining pillow
- [ ] Flashlight

DESK SUPPLIES

- [ ] Dictionary
- [ ] Thesaurus
- [ ] Computer
- [ ] Printer
- [ ] Toner cartridge
- [ ] Paper
- [ ] Legal tablets
- [ ] Sticky-back notes
- [ ] Letter holder
- [ ] Paper clips and holder
- [ ] Correction fluid
- [ ] Pens and pencils
- [ ] Stapler and staples
- [ ] Ruler
- [ ] Calculator
- [ ] Glue
- [ ] Thumbtacks
- [ ] Tape dispenser and tape
- [ ] Erasers
- [ ] Rubber bands
- [ ] Electric pencil sharpener
- [ ] Desk organizers
- [ ] Scissors
- [ ] Calendar
- [ ] Address book
- [ ] Stamps
- [ ] Bookends
- [ ] Stationery
- [ ] Pencil holder

BEDDING AND LINENS

- ☐ Pillow
- ☐ Pillowcases
- ☐ Sheets
- ☐ Blankets
- ☐ Towels
- ☐ Washcloths
- ☐ Beach towel
- ☐ Mattress pad

LAUNDRY SUPPLIES

- ☐ Iron
- ☐ Ironing board
- ☐ Drying rack
- ☐ Laundry bag
- ☐ Laundry hamper
- ☐ Laundry detergent
- ☐ Fabric softener
- ☐ Stain remover
- ☐ Starch

PERSONAL CARE ITEMS

- ☐ Sewing kit
- ☐ Tool kit
- ☐ Hair dryer
- ☐ Curling iron
- ☐ Electric rollers
- ☐ Comb
- ☐ Brush
- ☐ Shower basket or tote
- ☐ Shampoo
- ☐ Conditioner
- ☐ Toothbrush
- ☐ Toothpaste
- ☐ Soap

- ☐ Soap box
- ☐ Toothbrush box
- ☐ Razor
- ☐ Shaving cream
- ☐ Cotton balls
- ☐ Deodorant
- ☐ Cotton swabs
- ☐ First-aid kit
- ☐ Facial tissue
- ☐ Aspirin or pain reliever
- ☐ Safety pins
- ☐ Extra contact lenses or glasses
- ☐ Prescription for glasses
- ☐ Cosmetic organizer
- ☐ Extra prescriptions for personal medications

BASIC KITCHEN SUPPLIES

- ☐ Paper towels
- ☐ Can opener
- ☐ Coffee mug
- ☐ Paper plates
- ☐ Hot pot
- ☐ Popcorn popper
- ☐ Munchies jar or tin
- ☐ Knives, forks, and spoons
- ☐ Bathroom cup

CLOTHING

- ☐ Undergarments
- ☐ Socks
- ☐ Gloves
- ☐ Scarves
- ☐ Hats
- ☐ Winter coat

- ☐ Raincoat
- ☐ Lightweight jacket
- ☐ Jeans
- ☐ Slacks
- ☐ Shorts
- ☐ Workout clothes
- ☐ Jogging suits
- ☐ Swimsuit
- ☐ Dresses
- ☐ Skirts

- ☐ Blouses
- ☐ Shirts
- ☐ Sweaters
- ☐ Pajamas or nightgowns
- ☐ Shoes
- ☐ Boots
- ☐ Slippers
- ☐ Shower thongs
- ☐ Umbrella

Save Your Sanity on Special Occasions

In my family, special events were special for everyone but me. When we went on our annual vacation, I never felt rested or renewed. On Christmas Eve, I was way too tired from all the shopping, wrapping, and cooking to savor the seasonal goodies, not to mention staying awake for our church's magical midnight service. And I dreaded my kids' birthday parties. For weeks the planning would consume me and then, the big day would arrive. Two dozen (what was I thinking?) overactive kids would take over my house, have a great time, and leave me with a huge mess to clean up. I wished I could ban all future birthdays—not so my kids would stay little longer, but so I'd never have to endure another party again.

Then it dawned on me that my business background might serve me well in this department, too. In any organization, a special event—be it a sales conference or holiday party—needs to be managed. And each requires careful follow-through until it comes to a close. Applying the same strategies a company uses—planning, research and development, delegation, and deadlines—works for birthdays, vacations, holidays, and family reunions.

As your family's Family Manager, you're likely the one who organizes and coordinates the special events in your family's life. These projects might be small or large, once-in-a-lifetime or annual affairs. They're called "special" because

"People need joy quite as much as clothing. Some of them need it far more."
—Margaret Collier Graham

they're important memory-makers not to be missed. But like anything else in life that is significant, they take time and work to pull off.

At home as well as the office, planning something big usually requires the help of other people. I decided that if I needed an accountant, I would hire an accountant. If I wanted to add a room to our house, I would call a builder. So if I needed some help with pulling off a party, I could share the load. When family members assist with cooking, decorating, errands, invitations, reservations, etc., it's a huge load off Mom. Because I was no longer responsible for handling the whole thing by myself, I could enjoy it more. And probably at your house, like at mine, when Mom's having a good time, everybody's having a good time.

Making Occasions Special

Because planning for special occasions or vacations is something extra added to your already-too-long to-do list, it's easy to get tired, stressed out, and wonder why you're doing it in the first place. Just remember, there's something bigger going on than icing the forty-ninth cupcake or trying to cram a baby stroller, portacrib, and portable swing into your car so you can spend a leisurely week camping out. You're making memories. You're helping create opportunities for your family to get to know each other better and enjoy life together. You're carrying on traditions. That's big.

> "We find in life exactly what we put in it."
> —Ralph Waldo Emerson

You won't find a more worthwhile investment opportunity than your own family. And the payback, although sometimes slow in coming, more than makes up for any sacrifice you made. Remember: Anything you buy with money will wear out; anything you buy with love will last a lifetime.

Let's face it: Our kids won't remember how many school lunches we packed, uniforms we washed, or errands we ran for them. They will remember the party you threw to applaud a great report card, the family trip to a dude ranch, the big bash you threw for Grandma and Grandpa's anniversary. Times like these are crucial to a family's culture and cohesion— and joy.

> "Do what you can, with what you have, where you are."
> —Theodore Roosevelt

Here are some tips for making special occasions a fun and successful effort for everyone—even the Family Manager!

- **Watch for steps in the planning and execution process family members can do together.** As you work on special events, remind yourself that the process is part of it. It's as much as about working together toward a common end—in harmony and with humor—as it is about the event itself.

- **Cut yourself some slack.** Your goal is to make memories, not ulcers. Let perfectionism go, be enthusiastic, and focus on fun.

- **Don't let budget constraints hold you back.** If you wait until you "have enough money," you might wait forever! Let creativity fill in the cracks. You'll be amazed at what some imagination can do—it often delivers far more than mere finances can.

- **When an idea or attempt flops, don't despair.** Laugh. Some attempts will fail. Set a smart example by appreciating the absurdity of the moment and laughing instead of moaning. After all, flops make memories, too—sometimes even the best ones!

- **Think through the what-ifs.** Envision what you would do if you're at the lake for a Labor Day picnic and your child falls into the lake and gets soaking wet. What will you do if a thunderstorm comes suddenly while you're barbecuing chicken in the backyard for a Welcome Summer bash? Contingency planning can mean the difference between chaos and calm.

- **Practice advance work.** Think through the steps you need to take for the event to be a "best case scenario." A friend of ours was on the White House advance team. He traveled to cities a few days before the president and made sure all the details were handled so the president would have a smooth, trouble-free visit. As the Family Manager, you oversee necessary advance work for the small and the large family events. If it's a birthday party, what's your theme? Where can you get the décor? Will you buy or bake a cake? Will it be a layer cake or an ice-cream cake? Don't leave details until the day—or even the week—before.

> "A good plan today is better than a perfect plan tomorrow."
> —General George Patton

Holiday Dates

Use this list to remember upcoming holidays or to choose ones that sound interesting. Once you and your family agree on which days to highlight, research what each is all about to get ideas about how to honor the day.

New Year's Day	**January 1**
Feast of the Magi	January 6
Martin Luther King Day	**Third Monday in January**
Inauguration Day	January 20
Chinese New Year	**Between January 21 and February 19**
National Freedom Day	February 1
Groundhog Day	**February 2**
Lincoln's Birthday	February 12
Valentine's Day	**February 14**
Washington's Birthday	February 22
Ash Wednesday	**Late February**
President's Day	Third Monday in February
St. Patrick's Day	**March 17**
First Day of Spring	March 21
Passover	**March or April (14th of Nisan)**
Palm Sunday	Sunday before Easter
Good Friday	**Friday before Easter**
Easter	March or April
Easter Monday	**Monday after Easter**
April Fool's Day	April 1
Pan American Day	**April 14**
Earth Day	Third Sunday in April
Arbor Day	**Last Friday in April**
Professional Secretaries' Week	Fourth Week in April
May Day	**May 1**
National Day of Prayer	First Thursday in May
National Teacher Day	**Tuesday of the first full week of May**
Cinco de Mayo	May 5
Mother's Day	**Second Sunday in May**

Armed Forces Day	Third Saturday in May
Victoria Day	**First Monday preceding May 25**
Memorial Day (observed)	Last Monday in May
Memorial Day	**May 30**
Flag Day	June 14
Father's Day	**Third Sunday in June**
First Day of Summer	June 21
Canada Day	**July 1**
Fourth of July	July 4
Bastille Day (French Independence)	**July 14**
Labor Day	First Monday in September
Grandparents' Day	**First Sunday after Labor Day**
First Day of Autumn	September 17
Citizenship Day	**September 21**
Succos (Jewish harvest festival)	September/October
Rosh Hashanah (Jewish New Year)	**September or October**
Yom Kippur (Day of Atonement)	September or October
Columbus Day	**Second Monday in October**
National Boss Day	October 16
Thanksgiving in Canada	**Second Monday in October**
Mother-in-Law's Day	Last Sunday in October
United Nations Day	**October 24**
Halloween	October 31
All Saints' Day	**November 1**
All Souls' Day	November 2
Election Day	**First Tuesday after the first Monday in November**
Veterans' Day	November 11
Thanksgiving	**Fourth Thursday in November**
Hanukkah	November or December
First Day of Advent	**December 1**
Christmas	December 25
Boxing Day	**December 26**
Kwanzaa	December 26 to January 1
New Year's Eve	**December 31**

Building Your Own Special Events Team

A Family Manager is usually the one who organizes and coordinates the special events, parties, and projects in her family's life each year. These projects may be small or large, once-in-a-lifetime or annual events. What they all have in common is that they fall outside the normal routine of daily activities. Birthdays, vacations, Christmas, and other holidays are all special projects, but so are building or remodeling a house and heading up a school or community fund-raiser. Each calls for a certain amount of planning, research, delegation, and meeting deadlines.

But you don't have to go it alone. Enlist family members as your special events team to help with the planning and preparation. If you want to get your family onboard, these tips will get the process started and help you be a great leader.

1. **Brainstorm with family members about events they'd like to celebrate.** Decide what's important to your family: certainly birthdays, graduations, and holidays are part of every family's calendar, but you don't have to place the same importance on them everyone else does. Each family is free to decide what days—no matter how "silly" or unexpected—they deem worthy of some streamers and balloons. Use the list of holidays on page 154 to help, and make a list.

2. **Get out your calendar.** Mark it, month by month, for the special occasions and events you know will occur—birthdays, holidays, weddings, etc. Then list the events you want to occur: an eightieth birthday party for Grandma, a family ski trip, a Super Bowl party, a Fourth of July neighborhood barbeque. Once they're on the calendar, they serve to remind you to keep an eye out for menus, party items on sale, and so on.

3. **Consider special events penned—not penciled—on your calendar.** Once you've marked these events, don't let anyone talk you out of them. "Just say no" to invitations and demands that infringe on times you've designated as special for your family.

4. **Use Special Events Planner for each occasion.** This will help you think more clearly and feel less overwhelmed. This will also keep information in one place. When you see the tasks that need to be accomplished, items you need to buy, people you need to invite, etc., put them on the list. Then decide what you can delegate, what you might want to delete, and what you might want to do yourself. (You can download a free Special Events Planner template at www.familymanager.com.)

5. **Delegate and delete.** This is where you remind your family, "We're in this together." Working as a team promotes bonding, develops family spirit, and celebrates creative expression. So once you've roughed out a to-do list for a special event, call a family meeting. Ask for input and volunteers.

    Remember: You manage your family. You do not have to do things the way anyone else does—including your mother. So be bold: Are there some items on your list that really don't need doing? Can you buy a bakery cake instead of spending a whole weekend trying to make a cake the size and color of the Hulk? If you're hosting a holiday dinner for your extended family, can you ask others to bring some of the food? Or someone to come early and help set up? Or stay late and help clean up? Be generous in sharing the workload and in letting yourself off the hook.

6. **Conduct research and development.** To make an event all it can be, you might need to do some calling, some researching on the Internet, or some writing for information. Start collecting the information you need, such as rates for the hotel you'll need to stay at on the family vacation, dates a certain park area is available for your son's baseball-themed birthday party, the supplies needed for the baby shower you're throwing for your sister, etc.

    If others in your family are responsible for these tasks, give them deadlines and follow up to be sure everything gets done.

7. **Practice the five-minute maxim.** Watch for snippets of time here and there to accomplish something toward the occasion. For example, if you don't have a block of time to address all the party invitations, fill out a

few when you see a free five minutes. You'll eventually make it through the entire list.

8. **Execute and enjoy.** Now you get to enjoy the fruits of your labor: All the planning, purchasing, researching, packing, calling, inviting, and deciding prove their worth. Don't forget that special events are primarily to enjoy, not labor over. As the Family Manager, you set the tone. So let loose and have a great time!

9. **Appreciate your team and honor your own labor.** After the event is over, be sure to thank your family members for their contributions and feel the satisfaction yourself of adding another great memory to your family's account.

10. **Recap.** Talk together and make some notes about what worked and what didn't, and list ideas for next time. Take a lot of photos and take some family time to remember the day. Consider letting a creative family member compile a scrapbook or special photo album of the event.

Motivating Your Team

- Cheer your family members on in their efforts to help.

- Don't expect perfection, but shower praise for effort.

- Reward the completion of tasks in age-appropriate ways. Depending on the recipient, a cookie, an extra hour of television, or an evening with the car is important for your family's morale in addition to strengthening the teamwork system.

- Be a positive role model. To get enthusiasm, you have to give it.

- Look for ways to make jobs fun. Set a timer and see how fast kids can finish jobs.

- Be supportive and express confidence in your family's ability to do a good job. Your positive expectations create an atmosphere for better performance.

- Don't use guilt to motivate.

- Use gentle reminders to keep things moving. It might be obvious to you that the yard needs mowing a day early this week because of the potluck dinner you're hosting on Friday night, but your husband might be focused on other things. Don't approach team members when you feel resentful and overworked.

- Ask for team members' opinions. You'll bolster their self-esteem and inspire their work.

- When putting together a timetable and assigning tasks, listen as well as talk.

- Ask instead of telling team members to do things.

- Remind team members how doing their work and making a special event truly special will benefit them. "What will it do for me?" is *not* an unreasonable question for a family team member to ask.

- Be realistic. Maybe your son didn't get the streamers strung because he got home late from basketball practice. Things will go wrong occasionally, and it's often no one's fault. Stay cheerful.

- Create anticipation by promising surprises, fun times, and even rewards for participation beyond the event itself.

Five Ways to Avoid a Party Headache "This Big"

- Focus your energy on the event. When you're busy with a special project, can you delegate daily chores to someone else? Maybe that's the time to reevaluate whether the kitchen floor really needs to be scrubbed once a week. You might let some daily chores slide for a week or two. You might even discover there are things you've been doing more frequently than you actually need to for your family's happiness and peace of mind.

- Ask your friends who've done a similar event for ideas. Be sure to ask: "What's the main thing you

> "It isn't the big pleasures that count the most; it's making a great deal out of the little ones."
> —Jean Webster

Spur-of-the-Moment Celebrating

Not every event has to be elaborate and pre-planned. You might decide at the last minute to throw a birthday party for your husband—who said he didn't want a party, but you could tell he did. Or you might decide to start a quick new tradition on St. Patrick's Day to celebrate your Irish heritage. Be celebration-ready so you can respond to sudden inspiration: Keep on hand various colors of balloons, streamers, candles, and poster board for signs. Sometimes the events that work the best are spontaneous and can become family traditions.

wish you'd known beforehand?" The hardest things to plan for are the things you don't know about.

- Remember to let family members, even the smallest of children, volunteer for some jobs. Work with people's strengths, and pitch in together to do the unpleasant parts that no one wants.

- Remember why you're doing all this work.

- No matter what goes wrong along the way, give credit where credit is due. Be sure to compliment and praise your team members for their effort. A happy team is a productive team.

Celebration Seven-Day Countdown

Whether you enjoy a simple meal with your immediate family or spread your table elaborately for many, holidays and special occasions can be more than opportunities for exhaustion. They can be times when you savor great food, shared joys, and true thanksgiving for the occasion and the people with whom you share it. Whether it's a Memorial Day cookout, your parents' fiftieth anniversary, or a New Year's Eve party, it's important to start early, share the work, and take simple shortcuts.

Here's a plan for pulling off a special occasion in only a week. On the day of the event, you'll be amazed what you were able to accomplish in a short period of time. Use these ideas for a Thanksgiving feast, Easter gathering, Fourth of July cookout, or anytime you wish you had a magic wand!

fnifi FamilyManager SPECIAL EVENTS PLANNER

OCCASION: _____ DATE: _____

TIME: _____ PLACE: _____

GUESTS	THEME IDEAS	FOOD/BEVERAGE	DECORATIONS/FAVORS

RSVP
☐ _____
☐ _____
☐ _____
☐ _____
☐ _____
☐ _____
☐ _____
☐ _____
☐ _____
☐ _____
☐ _____
☐ _____
☐ _____
☐ _____
☐ _____
☐ _____
☐ _____
☐ _____
☐ _____
☐ _____

CO-HOSTS/HELPERS	ACTIVITIES/GAMES	GIFTS/SHOPPING

NOTES

SEVEN DAYS BEFORE THE BIG EVENT

■ Plan your menu. Include as many make-ahead dishes as possible, and don't forget family favorites. Don't knock yourself out fixing winter-squash-and-kumquat pie when plain apple pie is what everyone wants. Fruit salad doesn't have to be in a fancy mold to be festive. And it's just plain smart to buy things that the bakery or deli can make better than you can.

■ Make your own checklist or use the Family Manager Special Events Planner. Divide tasks among able family members. Write family members' initials by their tasks, and post the list in a central location.

■ Make a guest list, then phone or e-mail guests to invite them. Be sure to ask for RSVPs. If you're inviting extended family or close friends, consider assigning parts of the meal and let people contribute what they're good at fixing.

■ Check to see if you have enough dishes: dinner plates, dessert plates, coffee cups and saucers, silverware, glasses. Do the same with napkins. It's perfectly fine to use paper dishware for festive occasions to make cleanup simple. If the occasion calls for fine china, consider hiring someone to help clean up so you can enjoy your guests.

■ Check to see how you're doing on bakeware, serving dishes, platters, bread baskets, and such. Now is the time to buy or borrow to get what you need.

■ Cut yourself some slack. Consider hiring a responsible teenager to run errands, grocery shop, clean house, or play with the kids while you bake or work on decorations.

SIX DAYS BEFORE

■ Carefully check recipes and your list of who's bringing what, then make your grocery list.

■ Relieve your refrigerator of unnecessary items to make room for special-event foods. Ditto for your freezer.

FIVE DAYS BEFORE

- Shop for groceries, as well as film and batteries for your camera.

- When putting away groceries, organize foods in your pantry and refrigerator according to recipe.

- Buy kids' craft items for keeping young cousins and friends creatively occupied on the day of the event (see "Fast, Creative Ideas for Kids' Holiday Fun, page 169).

- Delegate someone to be in charge of helping kids with crafts while you're in the kitchen.

- Start making foods that you can freeze for side dishes or portions of recipes.

- Plan your centerpiece.

FOUR DAYS BEFORE

- Check napkins and tablecloths. Launder and iron if needed. Spray with fabric protector for easier cleanup of spots and spills.

- If you're feeding a crowd, count chairs and tables and round up extras from the patio, friends, or a rental company.

- Write a timetable of what needs to be done when on the event day. Start with what time you want to eat and work backward. What should you prepare first? How long will it take to get the grill going and barbecue the chicken? How big is your turkey, and how long should it cook? What's the last thing you want to take out of the oven? Schedule in some time to relax, too!

- Be sure you have enough burners and pots for cooking and warming right before dinner. Think about what dishes could be warmed in the microwave. A slow cooker can also serve as a warmer.

- Fix one or two dishes you can freeze.

THREE DAYS BEFORE

- Scout serving pieces you'll use, and check glassware and china. Clean or polish as needed.

- Make more space for food preparation by clearing off kitchen countertops and storing anything you won't need.

- Fix one or two dishes you can freeze.

TWO DAYS BEFORE

- Plan seating arrangement. Make place cards if you're hosting a big crowd.

- Set the table and arrange your centerpiece.

- Fill salt and pepper shakers.

- Start storing ice in bags in your freezer.

- Fix one or two dishes you can freeze or serve cold.

THE DAY BEFORE

- If you need some uninterrupted kitchen time, ask a friend to watch your kids for a couple hours. Repay the favor when she's having a party.

- Defrost frozen dishes.

- Prepare any dishes you couldn't freeze.

- Buy bread and flowers.

- Give your house a quick once-over.

- Chill wine.

- Make room in the closet for guests' coats.

- Set the table.

THE BIG DAY

- Carry out your event-day timetable.

- Enjoy yourself!

■ Start a special events notebook. Include your Special Events Planner, what you served and the recipes, who attended, activities, and so on. Record what did and didn't work. You'll save time and trouble year after year!

Birthdays

Children's parties are becoming more and more elaborate—from hiring magicians or clowns, to backyard petting zoos, outings at skateboard parks, or even parties at pizza places with indoor playgrounds. On the one hand, it's wonderful to have so many fun options, but on the other, many moms report feeling pressured to keep up.

Before the stress of planning the next birthday gets to you, keep in mind that most children are happy with the basics: a few presents to open, some friends to share the day with, and a special cake just for them.

Regardless of the type of party you're throwing, if you plan in advance, get input from your child, and come up with a manageable guest list, it will be a success—and you won't go nuts in the process. Here are tips for making your child's day special and some tips for making your job easier. Remember, in the end, your goal is happy children, not impressed adults.

> **"Memory is more indelible than ink."** —Anita Loos

Better Birthday Parties

■ Plan ahead. Begin planning a month in advance, especially if you're hiring entertainment or renting equipment. Ask around for referrals from neighbors and friends. A less-expensive option may be to hire a teenager or two to amuse your guests.

■ Determine how much you can afford to spend and how many children your child can invite. (The general rule is that the number of guests should equal the child's age, but that

The Ties That Bind

There's just something about being able to say, "This is the way our family always does it" or "Remember when . . . That was hilarious!" Traditions and common experiences cement a family together. Every child's mind is a curator of memories. Fun family times and special traditions go a long way in building a rich museum of positive remembrances for our children.

Special projects—traditions, holidays, and celebrations unique to your family—bind you to each other. These are the times when you can laugh, love, and enjoy life together—three things everyone needs large doses of.

doesn't always work. Some children don't enjoy the chaos of a large crowd. In that case, two to three friends might be the perfect party.) Keep in mind that if you're planning a party for two- or three-year-olds, you'll need to invite a parent, too. This will help the kids feel more comfortable and provide extra hands for games and refreshments, but you'll need to provide refreshments for the adult crowd as well. Between six and eight kids this age is plenty! Four and five-year-olds need lots of energy-busting activities. Eight to ten of them will be all you can handle unless you have help. Because six-year-olds are fairly independent and capable of helping during the party, you can handle more of them. Invite eight to twelve. Plan to have a party assistant—your husband, a friend, an older child—to help with younger children's celebrations. Or hire a responsible teenager to help with preparations, picture-taking, and cleanup.

- Encourage kids who are old enough to use My Own Party Planner. (Download My Own Party Planner at www.familymanager.com.) Work together on the brainstorming and details.

- Be sensitive to hurt feelings when putting together your guest list. Don't neglect new children in the neighborhood. If possible, invite a school-age child's entire class. If the class is too large, explain to your child why having everyone won't work out, and mail invitations to the guest's home addresses (instead of distributing them in class) so no one feels left out.

- Let your child's age determine the length of the party. The younger the child, the shorter the party. A sixty- to ninety-minute celebration is just right for two-year-olds. Older kids can handle two to three hours of partying. A length of a party for teenagers might depend on parental tolerance for late hours and loud music. Negotiate the length of the party beforehand with your teen.

- Come up with several themes for the birthday girl or boy to choose from or ask the child for ideas. You can build a party around almost anything your child has an interest in.

- Select a kid-friendly location. Home is always a wonderful choice, if you have room to accommodate the guests. It can be the most convenient place,

MY OWN PARTY PLANNER

NAME:

EVENT: DATE:

What kind of party do I want to have? List choices:

1. _____

2. _____

3. _____

Where do I want to have the party? List choices:

1. _____

2. _____

3. _____

Friends I want to invite:

_____ _____

_____ _____

_____ _____

_____ _____

_____ _____

Food:

_____ _____

_____ _____

Decoration and party favor ideas:

_____ _____

_____ _____

_____ _____

Activities, crafts, and/or games:

_____ _____

_____ _____

_____ _____

PARENT CHECKLIST

❑   Confirm date: _____

❑   Set time: _____

❑   Reserve place: _____

       _____

❑   Send invitations: _____

Food & beverages

❑   _____

❑   _____

❑   _____

❑   _____

❑   _____

Decorations & Party Favors

❑   _____

❑   _____

❑   _____

❑   _____

Games & Activities

❑   _____

❑   _____

❑   _____

❑   _____

❑   _____

Shopping List

❑   _____

❑   _____

❑   _____

❑   _____

❑   _____

❑   _____

too, because you don't have to transport supplies. The downside, of course, is the preparation and cleanup. But parties outside the home can be pricey. Most places geared toward birthday parties start at more than $10 per child, and that usually doesn't include goodie bags. Less-expensive options worth looking into might include renting a room at your town's library or community center. A warm-weather party could take place at a public pool or playground.

■ Decide what foods to serve. Be mindful of choking hazards for kids three and under (hotdogs, popcorn, and grapes are generally considered no-nos). The easiest way to do food is to avoid serving a meal by having the party in the late afternoon between lunch and dinner. That way juice, cake, ice cream, and a few treats to snack on can make up the menu. Throw a mid-morning party for two- and three-year-olds, however. That way the party won't inter-fere with naps, kids are less likely to be cranky, and you can serve no-fuss food such as donuts, bagels, and cream cheese (don't forget coffee for the moms).

■ Choose and buy supplies for some simple crafts kids can do while everyone is arriving. Set out markers and crayons, hang butcher block paper, and let them draw on the wall. Fashion jewelry from Fruit Loops or Gummy Life-savers and shoe-string licorice. Making a placemat is another simple craft that is a hit with kids any age. Make color copies of illustrations from a fa-vorite book and provide pre-cut poster board and glue. Have the kids glue and arrange the illustrations on the poster board, write their names on it, then you, a spouse, or a helpful friend can protect the masterpiece with a piece of contact paper.

■ Consider making your own invitations. Your son or daughter might enjoy helping with this, and if you have a home computer it's a cinch. Send them out at least two weeks before the party. Be sure to put RSVP on the invitation.

■ On party day, make each guest feel special. Put a smiling greeter at the front door to welcome children as they arrive.

■ Consider using an instant-develop camera to create party souvenirs. Take a snapshot of each guest in the midst of merrymaking and send it home with the child.

■ Have party guests sit in a circle holding their present. Let birthday child spin a bottle to see whose gift he will open. Have that guest sit next to the honoree. Take their photo when gift is opened. Repeat process.

■ Encourage your child to write thank you notes to his guests, even if he thanked them at the party. It's a great habit to start for lifelong courtesy (see Teaching Good Manners page 115).

Fast, Creative Ideas for Kids' Holiday Fun

For kids, fun activities help make fun memories. Here are some fast, creative, and inexpensive ideas you can pull out of your hat to help make a holiday special in kid-terms:

New Year's. Help kids make a giant clock from poster board for the countdown to midnight. Use a metal brad to secure movable clock hands. Let younger children move the hands corresponding to the correct time. Get the clock out year after year. It will get tattered, but it's a great keepsake and memory.

Groundhog Day. Make groundhog puppets. Use a brown crayon or marker to color the outside of a white, 10-ounce Styrofoam cup. With a pencil, poke a hole the size of a plastic drinking straw in the center bottom of the cup. Color a 2-inch Styrofoam ball to look like the head of a groundhog, and glue small felt pieces on the ball for facial features and ears. Push one end of a straw into the neck part of the head and the other end of the straw through the hole in the cup. Holding the cup right-side up, pull the straw down; the groundhog's head will disappear inside the cup. Push the straw up and down to pretend the groundhog is coming out of its hole.

Valentine's Day. Have a treasure hunt every year on Valentine's Day morning. Give your children the first clue, which leads to another clue somewhere in your home. Make up about five or six clues, with the last one leading them to a gift.

Presidents' Day. Have family members collect interesting trivia about presidents and come to the dinner table prepared to stump other family members with their questions. For example, who was the first U.S. president to have a telephone on his desk? (The answer is Herbert Hoover. Prior to 1929, the president used a telephone booth outside his office.) Have a prize for the winner.

St. Patrick's Day. Have children wrap pennies in gold foil, then Mom or Dad can hide them in a sandbox or grassy area of your yard. Children can pretend to be leprechauns and search for the golden nugget pennies. Allow children five minutes to find all the pennies they can, which they can keep for prizes.

You can also fill a jar with green jelly beans and have family members guess how many beans are in the jar. Whoever guesses closest to the actual number of jelly beans gets the jelly beans and chore relief for a day or two.

First Day of Spring. Celebrate the end of winter by visiting a park and playing this string puzzle game. Using a long ball of string, tie the loose end to a starting point. Walk the path you want your children to take, unraveling the string as you go. Put a treat or reward at the end of the string. Beginning at the starting point, let your children follow the course of the string and wind it back into a ball as they go.

April Fools' Day. Pack something silly in your child's sack lunch, such as an apple with a candy gummy worm sticking out of the side. Let your children trick their friends with a box of baby rattlers. Put several baby rattle toys in a medium-size box with a lid. Attach a sign to the outside of the box that says: DANGER! BABY RATTLERS INSIDE.

Winter Solstice. Make yarn snowflakes. Dip a 36-inch length of yarn into white glue. Arrange the yarn in a snowflake shape on a piece of waxed paper. When the yarn is dry, peel the snowflake away from the waxed paper. Paint a light coat of glue on each side of the snowflake, and sprinkle it with glitter. Make a hanger from a loop of thread or dental floss, and hang the snowflake in a window.

Easter. Make confetti eggs. Using a metal skewer or the end of a potato peeler, make a nickel-size hole in one end of a raw egg. Drain the egg white and yolk, and rinse the empty shell with cool water, allowing it to dry in the carton hole-side down. Dye the eggs, then let them dry. Use a funnel to fill the shells with confetti, glue a round piece of tissue paper over the hole to seal it, and let your kids have confetti egg wars in the backyard. (Play "rake up the mess" when the war is over!)

Arbor Day. Create twig baskets. Cut about two dozen twigs. The twigs should be about ¼-inch wide and slightly taller than an empty, 12-ounce orange juice can. Use a low-temperature glue gun to secure twigs around the outside of the can. Make sure twigs are glued as close together as possible. When twigs are set in place, tuck small bits of Spanish moss into spacers between the twigs to fill holes where the can is showing. Use a wooden pick to push the moss between the twigs. Wrap a piece of raffia around the twigs, and tie it into a bow. The basket is pretty by itself, or it can be used to hold pencils or flowers.

May Day. Make flower piñatas for party favors for any party in May. Blow up a small balloon until it's about 5 inches in diameter; tie it at the neck. Cut newspaper into 1-by-8-inch strips; dip each strip into a bowl of liquid starch. Place wet newspaper strips on balloon until entire surface of balloon is covered, except for a 1-inch square opening around the knot. Let balloon dry. Repeat this process, adding one more layer of newspaper. Allow paper to dry completely. Stick a pin through the opening, pop the balloon, and remove it.

Cut out dozens of 2-inch scalloped circles from various colors of crepe paper. Glue the centers of the circles to the outside of the paper piñata, overlapping the circles, and completely cover the piñata. Pull up the outside edges of each circle to create a flower effect. Fill the piñata with candies and small plastic toys. Seal the hole with a crepe-paper flower.

Fourth of July and other patriotic holidays. Let kids help make a stars-and-stripes centerpiece and patriotic placemats. Buy white candles and red and blue nonflammable slick pen paints. (Ask your local craft store for the kind of slick pens used to decorate T-shirts.) Stick candles into a Styrofoam square to secure. Starting two-thirds of the way down, draw red lines down the sides of the candles to the bottom; draw tiny blue stars around the top one-third. Allow the candles to dry for two hours, then surround with greenery.

For placemats, cut white poster board into 18-by-13-inch rectangles for each.

Next, cut five 1½-by-18-inch strips of red construction paper for each placemat. Glue the red strips horizontally on each rectangle, 1½ inches apart, to make stripes. Cover the mats with a clear contact paper, or take them to an office supply shop and have them laminated. Buy dark blue napkins at the grocery or party supply store. Let kids paint small stars all over the napkins with a white paint pen. (Be sure to let napkins dry before using.) When setting the table, position the napkin horizontally in the upper left corner of the placemat so it looks like a flag.

Columbus Day. Make trading beads from bread dough. (When Columbus landed in the New World, he gave the island natives red caps and strings of beads.) Cut and discard the crust from ten slices of fresh, white bread. Shred the bread slices into a large bowl. Work in enough white school glue to form a soft dough. One at a time, shape dough into ½-inch beads. Store the unused dough in an airtight container to prevent drying. Make a hole through the center of each bead with a toothpick. Spread beads on waxed paper so they don't touch; let them dry overnight. Paint designs on the beads with acrylic paint. After they're dry, string the beads with fishing line to make a necklace.

Halloween. Buy tiny decorative pumpkin gourds, and let your child make faces and decorate them with a black indelible marker. (Wear old clothes when doing this.) Let them decorate their rooms with the tiny pumpkins.

Thanksgiving. Do-it-yourself tablecloth: Cover a child's table with white craft paper. Supply markers; help kids make handprint turkeys. Trace the outline of each child's hand on the paper. Make the thumb into the turkey's head and the fingers into feathers; add feet at the bottom of the palm. Kids can color their turkeys with markers. Be sure the kids wear aprons or smocks.

They can also have a turkey hunt: Have children draw or cut out ten to fifteen pictures of turkeys. Hide them around the house. The child who finds the most turkeys gets a prize.

Hosting a Great Family Gathering

In this age of supermobility, it's too easy to lose touch with extended family. When that happens, we actually lose more than regular contact—we miss out on traditions, memory-making, and enjoying the comforting bonds of kin.

To keep this from happening, we need to make family get-togethers a regular special event. The adventure of planning a reunion, whether a yearly occasion or something we're arranging for the first time, can really be fun. The following tips will help simplify the project so you can enjoy the reunion, too.

Planning

- Decide what type of reunion you'd like to have: a backyard barbecue for twenty to fifty family members; a weekend reunion held at a camp, resort, or hotel for fifty to two hundred family members; or a weeklong camping excursion in which twenty to eighty family members gather. Calculate the cost per individual/family for each idea.

- If desired, choose a theme or event to celebrate: someone's significant birthday, anniversary, or pivotal family event.

- Make it easier and more fun: Ask another family member to share the responsibilities.

- Set a date. You should begin planning a year before the reunion. Although you won't find a date that fits everyone's schedule, talk with a few key family members who will definitely attend, and set the most accommodating date you can. Or consider sending out a letter that asks about each family's availability.

- While you're discussing dates, ask around about activities everyone might enjoy, who might like to help plan, and so on.

- Consider what locations might work well: state or city parks, recreational clubs, scenic spots such as lakes. Call or write for information on each possible meeting place. Be sure the one you choose offers opportunities for everyone—a place to play softball, walk, swim—as well as wheelchair accessibility if needed.

■ Create a notebook or file folder that will hold all pertinent details: What must be bought, who's bringing what, list of those who have RSVP'ed, their housing arrangements, what you will do each day of the reunion and when.

■ Make realistic reservations: If the event requires a large per-family fee, plan on fewer to attend than you hope. If your day will be relatively inexpensive, overestimate attendees. Play it safe—base your reservation on the monies you've already collected, not those you hope to collect.

■ Notify family members well in advance with a detailed letter that lists the date, location, and other information. Include:

How much money each attendee will need to pay, and when, for expenses.

A questionnaire that asks all about the family as well as for a recent family photo. You'll copy and compile this info into a booklet that will let family members get acquainted before they meet again. (If you choose to get T-shirts printed for the reunion, ask for shirt sizes.)

A list of any special supplies, such as hats for the crazy-hat contest, instruments for a family band, or necessary props for a talent show.

■ Assign who will bring what—beverages, meat dishes, salads, desserts, and paper plates and silverware.

■ Assign cleanup teams. Consider also appointing a reunion photographer, children's playtime organizer, song leader, adult activity director, video-camera operator, family historian, etc.

A few weeks before the reunion, start talking as a family about who you will see and what you'll do. This will help young children know what to anticipate. If possible, get out photos of out-of-town family. Seeing pictures will help your family remember names and faces of people you haven't seen in a while.

■ Two weeks before the reunion, send a letter confirming details and adding any last-minute information. You might suggest that family members work together to create fun matching name tags to wear at the reunion.

■ If you don't ask families to bring their own, make name tags or have them ready for families to make themselves when they arrive.

Reunion Activities

■ Start with a game that will get family members mixing. A good get-to-know-you game is to list each family member's name on the left-hand side of a piece of paper. Copy the list, distribute them as people arrive, then give the group a set amount of time to find as many family members as they can. Beside each person's name, they should list when that person last went on vacation, the most fascinating experience he or she had in the last six months, and what he or she likes most to do during free time. The person who obtains the most answers wins a photo album.

■ An artistic family member can bring a large picture of a family tree—drawn perhaps on the back of an appliance box. Allot time for folks to write their families' names on branches.

■ Crazy-hat contest: Set a time for everyone to model his or her hat. Vote on who should receive a prize for the most unique, cutest, largest, ugliest, and most practical.

■ Commemorate the event by designing a T-shirt that everyone can wear during the reunion. Use the family questionnaire to collect sizes before you buy shirts.

■ Honor older family members. Have them describe the biggest world change of their lifetime, the happiest memory of their childhood, and the first home they remember.

■ Hold a family Olympics by dividing into teams and competing in these events: croquet, an egg toss, a three-legged race, badminton, or Ping-Pong. Each winner gets a fun prize.

■ Personalize colorful, inexpensive, plastic glasses with permanent paint pens. Write on each, for example: "Hawkins Family Reunion—2004." These serve as fun souvenirs as well as tableware.

Ask relatives to clean out their attics and basements before the reunion and bring some items they would like to auction off. Use the proceeds to defray the cost of next year's reunion.

- Appoint an interested family member to be reunion journalist: He or she should collect historical information and interesting facts throughout the event. Afterward, gather this info into a family newspaper that commemorates the day. Print and distribute to all who attended. Also consider compiling a family cookbook.

- Each family member should write a little-known fascinating fact about him- or herself on an index card. Collect the cards and have someone read each out loud to see if players can identify who wrote them.

- For kids, set up a game and craft area.

- Have a family talent show or band.

- Relive family history by reviewing family members' photo albums.

- Have older family members model vintage clothing. Give an award for the most memorable outfit.

- At the day's end, award family members for having the least amount of hair, the worst sunburn, the best laugh, or being the Queen of Potato Salad.

Tips for Taking Great Photos

Use these tips to be sure you record all those memories:

- Invest in a good camera. If you have a computer, consider a digital camera.

- Know how to use your camera before the event. Whether it's a new camera or an old one, glance over the owner's manual to be sure you know how to load and unload film and batteries.

- Keep an extra set of batteries on hand at home. Bring an extra set along when you're traveling. Batteries in tourist locations can be expensive and hard to find. Ditto with film. You don't want to miss the first time your child rides a merry-go-round.

- Use high-speed film so lighting is less critical.

- Shoot more face, less feet.

- Give your subjects time to relax before you press the shutter.

- Get down on kids' level to photograph them.

- Experiment with light for different effects. Professional photographers say that the best time to photograph is just after sunrise and just before sunset. Early and late light warms colors and adds softer shadows. Noon light creates dramatic shadows.

- Capture spontaneous expressions rather than posed smiles.

- Avoid harsh shadows by photographing people away from walls.

- Be sure your background doesn't overwhelm the people you're photographing. Use a field or the sky.

- Look for unusual angles. Lie on the grass for a shot of your kids playing croquet.

- To avoid the disappointing picture in which subjects closed their eyes the minute you clicked the shutter, make a noise just before pressing the button.

- When photographing a group, avoid a stacked look by staggering the heights in the back row.

- Shoot from different angles. Get above them and shoot down, or vice versa.

- Use your flash even when you don't think you need to. Your subjects will appear more distinct.

- Avoid red eyes in photographs by adding light in the room: Switch on lamps and pull window coverings. You can also ask your subject to glance at a bright light just before you take the photo.

- Get a picture with a soft effect by wrapping toilet tissue around your flash.

- Heavier folks will photograph better if you ask them to show their teeth when they smile and to gently stick out their chins while standing up straight and still.

- It might seem obvious, but be sure your subject is in the center of the picture.

- Photograph dark objects in front of a light background and vice versa.

- When photographing groups, don't stand them all an equal distance from the camera. Put a few closer and a few farther away.

- Press the shutter button gently—don't jerk.

- Ask subjects to wear bright clothes.

Creative Gifts for Special Occasions

Quick Gift Baskets

Whether it's Christmas, a birthday, graduation, or just time for a thank you, gift baskets are great. Line a pretty box or basket with bandannas or various colors of tissue paper, then fill with theme-related items. Your basket can be as simple or extravagant and as large or as small as your budget and creativity allow. Here are some ideas to get you started:

Athlete's basket: balls (golf, tennis, or racquetballs), socks, deodorant, sweatbands, energy bars, and a sports magazine

Beauty basket: fingernail polish, hair ornaments, bubble bath, lotion, a manicure set, and a makeup bag

Camper's basket: beef jerky or granola, mosquito repellent, a small first-aid kit, a pocket knife, a flashlight, and an astronomy book

Car-care basket: a large sponge, glass cleaner, chamois cloth, car wax, a travel coffee mug, a new key chain, an ice scraper, and a whisk broom

College survival basket: a roll of quarters, a mug and instant cocoa mix, candy bars, chewing gum, highlighter pens, pencils, and other study supplies

Craft-lover's basket: items for the types of crafts the recipient enjoys, such as painting, woodworking, or embroidery

Dog-lover's basket: dog biscuits, a rubber toy, a new collar, a package of chew sticks, and a bandanna

Fisherman's basket: hooks, lures, a jar of bait, flies, fishing line, needle-nose pliers, and a fishing magazine

Kitchen-lover's basket: spices, a fun-shape timer and/or other kitchen gadgets, new measuring cups and spoons, gourmet spices, and a cookbook (Instead of a basket, use a colorful colander, an unusual-shape cake pan, or pretty bowl or platter. Line it with tea towels or cloth napkins.)

Newlyweds' basket: handy household items such as tools, picture hangers, twine, refrigerator magnets, and a small book on home repair

Outdoor enthusiast's basket: waterproof sunscreen, compass, flashlight, bungee cords, snacks, waterproof matches, and a water bottle

Sewing basket: a package of needles, iron-on patches, small scissors, thread, a thimble, tape measure, fusible webbing, straight pens, and a sewing crafts magazine

Shoe-care basket: shoelaces, buffing brush or cloth, leather cleaner, water repellent, polish, and shoe trees

Buying Your Children Gifts That Matter

Whether it's a birthday, graduation, or any time you give a gift to your child . . .

- **Look beyond their wish list.** You may not be doing your kids a favor by purchasing gifts on their list if they've seen only the items on TV commercials. Ask yourself, What are my children's needs? At their current state of development—physical, emotional, intellectual—what else should be on their list? Incorporate some of these items along with your children's desires.

- **Look for toys that stimulate rather than entertain.** Beware of toys that tranquilize kids with mindless entertainment. Instead, choose gifts that encourage creativity and stimulate the intellect or senses.

- **Look for ways to provide experiences.** Consider giving lessons for special interests, such as arts and crafts, computers, music, or sports. Or give tickets to concerts, or travel money to visit family or friends.

- **Look for ways to emphasize the uniqueness of the child.** Celebrate your child's individuality by giving presents that correspond to his or her special gifts or talents.

Unusual Gifts

Tired of the same old gifts? Try these to spice up gift-giving!

For a young child: a day spent exploring the behind-the-scenes adventure at a fire station, a bakery, or a newspaper

For single moms or elderly folks: paint their home or clean their gutters

For the young parents: a gift certificate for dinner out while you watch the kids

For a special someone: a photo album full of meaningful pictures with the names and dates on the back of each

For close relatives: a family tree (Trace your family tree and make several copies. Frame them, and give to special family members.)

For immediate and extended family, or a future daughter-in-law: homemade recipe book (Ask family members for their best recipes; compile them to make a family cookbook.)

For a child or grandchild: heirloom gift (Surprise a loved one with something you would like to have handed down from generation to generation. This way he or she can enjoy it sooner rather than later.)

For a child or grandchild: cassette tape of bedtime stories or fairy tales you record yourself reading a child's favorite book or fairy tales

For the friend who is struggling financially: a gift certificate for a mass merchandise store (He or she can get an oil change or groceries.)

For the nostalgic: a newspaper from the honoree's birthdate

> To celebrate a special day in someone's life, send a letter and a self-addressed stamped envelope to friends of the honoree, asking them to write a warm greeting and send it back to you secretly. Collect the messages and present them to the honoree.

Gifts for Folks of Every Age

At some point, everyone hits the wall when shopping for presents. These will get you "unstumped" in a hurry.

KIDS

- A small plastic box of activities to do in the car

- Outerwear: rain gear, hat, mittens, sweatshirt, mittens, a colorful umbrella

- Subscription to a kids' magazine

- Book by a favorite author

- Athletic gear

- Beach or pool toys

- Gift certificates to a favorite fast-food or ice-cream shop

- A jewelry box full of sparkly plastic necklaces, rings, and bracelets

- Game or educational software

- Art supplies and a sketch pad

TEENS

- Blank book or book by a favorite author

- Tickets to a sports event or concert

- Camera

- Stationery

- A long-distance phone card

- Gift certificates for clothing stores

- Gift certificates for movie rentals

- Subscriptions to favorite magazines

Start a collection for each of your children. Add to it at Christmas and on birthdays.

- Tote bag

- Gift certificate to favorite "scent shop," where she can shop for bubble bath and cologne

- Gift certificate to music store

- Gift certificate to an athletic equipment store

FOR OLDER FOLKS

- A flashlight

- A daily calendar

- Scented lotion or talcum powder

- Gift certificates to bookstore, ice-cream shop, or coffee shop

- Handkerchiefs

- Stationery with stamps included

- A long-distance phone card

- An easy-to-care-for plant

- A music box

- A newspaper or magazine subscription

- A bulletin board and tacks for photos and reminders

- A photo album or videotape of your family (for grandparents and older relatives)

Religious Gifts

GENERAL PROTESTANT AND CATHOLIC

- A Bible with the recipient's name inscribed

- A cross necklace

- A devotional book

- A CD of inspirational music

FOR A BRIS

- A necklace bearing the chai, or Jewish symbol of life

- A mezuzah

- A silver Kiddush cup

- A tree planted in Israel (Write: Jewish National Fund, 42 East 69th St., New York, NY 10021 or call 800-542-8733)

FOR A CONFIRMATION OR FIRST COMMUNION

- A Bible

- A prayer book

- White gloves

- A book of children's devotions

- Jewelry engraved with the child's name

- A Bible-carrying case or cover

FOR A BAT/BAR MITZVAH

- Money gifts in increments of 18 (The chai, or Jewish symbol for life, stands for the number 18.)

- For boys, a tallis; for girls, tallis clips for a prayer shawl

- A menorah

- Shabbat candlesticks

- A copy of the Torah or Jewish Bible

- Jewelry bearing Star of David

- Embroidered yarmulke

- Matzo holder or seder plate

Plan the Best Vacation Ever

Research makes the difference between a trip that leaves you broke, exhausted, and resentful and one that lets you enjoy extras and come back refreshed and optimistic about future family vacations.

Long-Term Planning

- Work your vacation dates around everyone's busy schedule

- Choose your mode of transportation. If you're driving, plan to make long drives pleasant by stocking a cooler with drinks and snacks, bringing along music and books on tape, or packing a picnic.

- Search the Internet or write to the visitors' bureau or chamber of commerce in the state and city of your destination as well as the ones you will pass through. Ask for sightseeing brochures, a map, and info about lodging, local activities, and restaurants.

- Schedule a family meeting to talk about the trip budget and each member's expectations. Estimate the costs of different ideas, then prioritize the list.

"Never take a cross-country trip with a kid who has just learned to whistle." **—Jean Deuel**

- Consider using a travel agent or online travel service such as travelocity to research airfare, hotel, and car-rental options.

- If you'd like to stay at a campsite, dude ranch, or popular public park, make reservations now. These locales tend to book up early. If you'll be renting a house, condo, or vacation villa, make reservations now.

- Search for affordable lodging. Ask friends or travel agents for tips, and compare brochures. For each hotel, compare number of beds, baths, rooms, laundry and kitchen facilities, activities for children, baby-sitting services, and sport amenities.

- Be sure local restaurants have kids' menus.

- Be sure to ask about all discounts before you book a room.

- Read the fine print. Brochures and photos don't guarantee anything.

- Beware of travel packages that require a tour of resort property.

- Consider vacations at a national park.

- If you're renting a camper, make reservations now.

- Start a reading program for the trip. If kids meet their reading quota, they can earn a cash prize on the last day. (Reading fiction or nonfiction about the place you are visiting will build their excitement when they see the place in real life.)

- Encourge your kids to start earning spending money for the trip.

- Want a baby-sitter to accompany your family on vacation? Make arrangements now.

- Arrange for pet care while you're away.

> ## Vacationing Overseas
>
> - Find out whether you and the kids need immunizations.
>
> - Research what paperwork family members need such as passports or visas.

Short-Term Planning

■ Guarantee your room for late arrival, no matter when you plan to arrive.

■ Know the existing balance and credit limit on each of your cards.

■ Fill out a form at the post office to arrange a vacation stop on mail. Ditto for newspaper delivery.

■ Plan to start driving early. On longer trips, reserve motel rooms ahead.

■ Before the trip, plan your meals and make a shopping list for when you arrive. Bring small items like spices from home. Freeze a casserole ahead and transport it in a cooler.

■ Highlight your route on a map so kids can track your progress.

■ Get the car tuned up and check the air pressure in your tires.

■ Take along a book you can read aloud to the family before you go to bed at night. Choose one you can start and finish on the trip.

■ Get office clothes dry-cleaned while you're away.

■ Put household lights on timers.

■ Leave a casserole in the freezer at home so you'll have a meal almost ready when you get home. Plan to do your laundry at a Laundromat, where you can do it all at once, and sort the mail while you're waiting. And always build in a one-day buffer between returning home and going back to school and work.

The Night Before Vacation.

■ Place luggage, tickets, and other necessary documents near the door.

■ Call your airline to confirm flights and double-check departure times.

How to Pack Smart

These tips help ensure that you get where you're going with the right stuff:

■ If possible, take only clothes made of lighter, hand-washable fabrics

- Pack socks and belts inside shoes.

- Don't forget emergency items, such as medication for sunburns and stomach upset, or Band-Aids.

- Pack last what you'll need first, such as pajamas.

- Pack wrinkle-resistant clothing.

- Pack nylons into a self-sealing plastic bag to avoid snags.

- Have each family make a list of what he's taking. He can check off each item as he repacks it for going home. This list will also serve as an inventory of what's in each bag for claims purposes or in case luggage goes AWOL.

En-Route Money-Saving Methods

- Drink water with meals.

- Use your cell phone (depending on your plan) or the pay phone in the hotel lobby rather than the one in your room.

- Buy snacks somewhere other than the in-room refrigerator.

- Skip room service.

- Don't wait until you're running on fumes to buy gas so you can look for competitive prices. Check oil and tires occasionally.

- Take smaller versions of big-bottle products like shampoo.

- Button buttons, zip zippers, and close snaps on clothes before packing. They'll retain their shape better.

- Squeeze excess air from bottles and tubes before sealing. You'll have fewer leaks.

- Assemble kids' clothes by complete day's outfit, and put each in a plastic bag. Choosing an outfit every day will be simple!

- Take along a small amount of laundry detergent for hand-washing and some clothespins. You can use these on hangers to dry clothes.

- If you're flying, take a just-in-case bag of daily medications, sewing kit, contact lens products, and so on. Consider adding a change of clothes.

- Take a large, plastic dirty-clothes bag and a collapsible bag for the souvenirs you buy.

- Take an electrical converter, if necessary.

Planning a Kid-Friendly Vacation

To be sure the kids have a great time, keep them in mind as you plan. Here are some tips:

- Be sure your destination has something for everyone. Let kids who are old enough help with planning.

- Do less than you think you can during the trip so no one comes home exhausted.

- Schedule alone-time for family members who need it.

- Don't expect kids to like the same things Mom and Dad do. Plan around the kids.

- Try something different: a bicycle tour, a family cruise, working at a guest ranch.

- Forget about the office. Focus on the family.

- Have your kids start a trip scrapbook, collecting things to put in each day such as postcards, a leaf, etc. Record humorous incidents and special memories.

- Make trip videos as you go, and watch them at night in your hotel. An older child could be in charge of making the video.

- Take advantage of local free entertainment: tours, museums, concerts.

■ At home, leave a copy of your itinerary, the numbers on your traveler's checks, credit cards you won't need, and copies of your passports/visas.

Flying High

To use air travel to your advantage. To trouble-proof your trip, use these tips:

■ Join frequent-flier programs. Some offer advance boarding privileges.

■ Look for discount tickets, but read the fine print.

■ Ask airlines or travel agents about discounts for families flying together.

■ Ask if land-air packages are available for your destination.

■ Try to make connections in a hub city rather than taking a more expensive non-stop flight.

■ Take several small individually wrapped toys to help the trip pass for small children.

■ Try to take flights that have movies—kids love this.

■ Bring along bottles of water and snacks in case you're thirsty or hungry before meals are served.

■ Try to arrive at the airport closest to your final destination.

■ Reserve bulkhead or emergency-exit seats for more legroom.

- Order kid-friendly meals at least twenty-four hours before departure time.

- Take some gum along for help unblocking ears during takeoff and landing.

- If traveling with a baby, take along enough formula, diapers, and other supplies. Be prepared for delays.

- Wear loose, comfortable clothing and shoes.

- Have each child bring a backpack of small toys and games.

- Put your name/address/phone number inside and outside your luggage.

- Tie a bright ribbon around handles of checked luggage to make them easily identifiable at baggage claim.

- Don't fly within twelve hours of having dental work.

- Ask for a pillow and blanket as soon as you're seated.

Twenty Ways to Save Your Sanity on a Road Trip

Days on the road can stretch too long for kids and adults. By planning ahead, you can save yourself from the bickering in the backseat—and the front.

- Decide on the agenda for your trip beforehand. You and your husband may have completely different ideas of what a road trip should entail. Talk about whether you want a highly scheduled lineup of activities or a relaxed, hang-loose kind of holiday. Getting unspoken expectations on the table before the trip will help omit conflict.

- Don't wait until the last minute to prepare. Share the many errands required before a trip: servicing the car, filling up with gas, installing the proper safety seats, and packing the night before you leave. Go to bed early if possible.

- Pack smart. Place pajamas, toothbrush, hairbrush—everything you

Packing Smart

Put anything that might leak in a self-sealing plastic bag. Put in extra plastic bags for wet swimsuits and such.

need for going to sleep—on top of your suitcase or in a separate bag so it will be ready for your first night at your destination.

- Let your child pack a travel box with small toys, art supplies, and other treasures. Add a couple new toys for surprise treats. A 13×9×2-inch metal cake pan with a lid doubles as a storage box and lap desk in the car.

- Pack your sense of humor and a positive attitude. This will help you survive bad weather, rude people, poor service, and a host of other inconveniences.

- Plan the end of your trip, too. Leave a meal in the freezer at home awaiting your arrival.

- Be sure kids' clothes are easy to get in and out of during restroom visits.

- Relieve last-minute stress by glancing at the Vacation Exit Checklist before you leave the house (see page 192).

- Bring along music and books on cassette or CD the whole family will enjoy. Also bring joke and brainteaser books. They come in handy if you have to wait to get your car repaired. They're also fun to read together while waiting for food to be served in a restaurant. It's also not a bad idea to rent a mobile DVD unit and bring along some kid-friendly DVDs to help the time pass in the car.

- Cut out the portion of a map with the highways you'll be traveling, then highlight the route with a yellow marker. Glue your map to a piece of cardboard and laminate it with clear contact paper. Kids will enjoy tracking your progress.

- Play Look for the License Plates. Make a photocopy of a U.S. map. Glue the map to a piece of cardboard, and cover it with clear contact paper. Every time you spot a license plate from a different state, color in the state with an erasable marker. When you arrive at your destination, count the number of states you marked. Wipe off the board and play the game again on the way home.

> Have a tote bag or small plastic crate in the car specifically for kids to put their socks and shoes in when they take them off.

■ Have the driver and the referee share responsibilities. If possible, let each parent be relieved of his or her duties at regular intervals. Interstate traffic may be a delightful change for one parent, whereas the other might have a fresh supply of patience for the backseat. When both parents are tired or a backseat catastrophe occurs, it might be a good time to stop for a snack, air out the car, change the seating arrangement, then resume the trip by playing a great audiotape you've been saving for an hour of desperation.

> Take along Colorforms for young children. They work great on windows.

■ Require a five- to ten-minute period of silence each hour. (This can be a real sanity-saver.)

■ Stop every two hours. Let each person have a turn deciding when to stop. For example, an eight-year-old might dictate that at 2:17 you'll stop for ice cream. When that time comes, go to the first place that offers some. Dad might determine that at 5:54 he wants to stop at the first bait store you see after that time.

■ Carry a small notebook to keep pertinent trip information. For future reference, take notes along the way about the places you enjoyed or that gave you good service such as gas stations, motels, and restaurants. Make note of negative experiences, too, so you won't make the same mistake twice.

■ Diversity keeps kids content—let them exchange toys, snacks, and seats during the trip.

■ Comfort is everything. Let kids visit restrooms frequently, and keep them well fed: Bagels and fruit are good car snacks.

■ Offer kids water while traveling rather than pop or juice. They like water less, so they'll drink less, and you'll visit restrooms—less!

■ Stop at points of interest along the way to your final destination. This makes the trip pass more quickly.

Map Mania

Use your vacation plans and a road atlas to brush up your kids' skills with geography, math, and research:

▪ Teach your kids how to read a map or atlas. As they begin to understand road systems, show them where you live and where you will have your vacation this year.

▪ Ask them to add up the miles between different points.

▪ Have them figure out what would be a shorter route between Point A and Point B. Ask them: How much farther would it be if we stopped at this certain point of interest? If we average 60 miles per hour, how long will it take to get there? How many rivers will we cross? What is the highest mountain we will cross?

▪ Define "point of interest" and have them observe these on the map. Have them investigate the ones that intrigue them at the library, in an encyclopedia, on the Internet, or by calling the chamber of commerce.

▪ Let kids choose five points of interest they'd most like to visit on your trip.

Vacation Exit Checklist

Avoid the "Did you lock the door?" panic once you've hit the road. Use this checklist to make sure it all gets done:

☐ Call airline or go to their website to confirm flights and double-check departure times and gates.

☐ Check to be sure you have tickets and that everyone over age fifteen has a photo ID.

☐ Be sure all bags and gear are in the car.

☐ Secure items you couldn't pack until the last moment (child's security blanket, favorite stuffed animal, pillows, toiletry items).

☐ Confirm that newspaper and mail have been stopped or will be picked up by a neighbor.

☐ Confirm arrangements for plant and pet care.

☐ Fill prescriptions to cover your time away.

☐ Pick up any spare keys you've hidden outside.

☐ Give your itinerary and phone numbers where you can be reached to a friend, relative, or neighbor in case of emergency. (It's also a good idea to leave a key with someone so he or she can check on your house while you're away.)

☐ Unplug coffeemaker, small appliances, TV, electronic equipment, and computers to protect them from power surges while you're gone.

☐ Check to see if the stove and oven are turned off.

☐ Remove milk and other perishables from refrigerator.

☐ Be sure refrigerator and freezer doors are securely shut.

☐ Wash dirty dishes and run disposal.

☐ Take out all garbage.

☐ Turn off water supply to washing machine and ice maker.

☐ Activate answering machine.

☐ Set thermostat and adjust water heater for vacation setting.

☐ Set automatic light timers and sprinkler system.

☐ Check to see that all windows and doors are secure.

☐ Be sure no valuables are visible from the windows.

☐ Arm security system.

☐ Exit and lock the doors as well as the garage door and any outside buildings.

Travel Safely

Maximize your personal safety with these tips:

■ Carry on—don't check—valuables such as a camera or jewelry.

■ Keep all medications with you—don't check them.

■ Stay alert. Pickpockets thrive in touristy areas.

■ Park only in lighted areas, away from Dumpsters or trucks.

■ Don't open a hotel door to anyone before checking through the peephole. Ask for ID or call the front desk to confirm that someone is an employee.

■ Lock all windows and doors, including doors between connecting rooms. If any locks don't work, get another room.

Smart Moves

- Avoid booking the last flight of the day. If it's canceled for some reason, you're stranded overnight.

- When traveling abroad, photocopy the information page of your passport. Carry a copy separately when you travel.

- Hang the "Do Not Disturb" sign whenever you leave the room. It will look occupied.

- Return to your room in the evening via the hotel's front entrance.

- Store valuables in the hotel safe.

- Note the number of doors between your room and the closest exit. You'll be able to find your way if an emergency strikes and the lights go out.

- Keep your room key within sight at all times.

- Carry with you a list of all credit card numbers and the issuers' toll-free numbers in case of loss or theft.

- Stay only in hotels that have dead-bolt locks and peepholes on their doors.

- Don't mention your room number where anyone can hear you.

- If someone seems to be following you, go to a house phone, or in an emergency, pull the fire alarm.

Save Your Energy

Every week I receive mail from women who say they're tired, frustrated, and burned-out. They talk about carpooling kids; working on school projects; helping their spouses; caring for aging parents; "doing for" co-workers, churches, and friends. They want to know how to feel better so they can—you guessed it—continue doing! I call it the Do-Wop Syndrome—that is, the *wop* of exhaustion and resentment you get from do, do, doing for others without ever doing for yourself.

When our own needs go unmet, our bodies get stressed and start reacting. Our minds race in turmoil, our emotions are erratic, and our spirits become discouraged. We are in no condition to nurture anyone else.

I should know. More than twenty years ago, when my oldest son was in kindergarten, my life was crazy. Instead of easing into the morning, I'd push the snooze button on my alarm and linger under the covers until I had just ten or fifteen minutes to get John dressed, fed, and driven to school in time for the 8:30 tardy bell. I'd jerk my poor child out of bed, throw some clothes on him, and hurry into the kitchen for "breakfast," which usually consisted of dry cereal because we were often out of milk.

After several months of stressful living (needless to say, the rest of the day un-

> "To keep a lamp burning we have to keep putting oil into it."
> —Mother Teresa

folded a lot like the morning), I realized I was creating chaos for my family. Then I realized it all started with me. You see, a good Family Manager has to manage herself first. I learned the hard way that self-management may very well be the most important department a Family Manager oversees, because if she lets this go by the wayside, all the other departments suffer as well. It's impossible to be physically exhausted, emotionally frazzled, and spiritually empty and still toggle everything else for which you're responsible. In other words, you have to be in good shape to give good shape to the rest of your life.

The next time you're tempted to think your own needs are not important, remember that you are the nexus—the hub—and that your family doesn't need a cranky, tired, resentful mother. Your husband and children need someone who can give freely and guide joyfully because she has resources from which to draw. She has kept her own reservoir full, and she feels happy and energetic. In this section, you'll find hundreds of ways to take care of *you* and become the woman, mother, and friend you've always wanted to be.

Living a Balanced Life

No matter how many careers we have, we have only one life. Balance helps us see that the different aspects of life—physical, emotional, mental, and spiritual—are in correct relationship to one another. As long as each aspect of life gets the attention it needs, no more and no less, we will be available to enrich others' lives as well as our own. And we will be capable of meeting the demands of our lives with all of the energy they require.

Here are five steps to implementing the beauty of balance in your life:

- **Know what drains and replenishes you emotionally, and know how to find middle ground between the two.** When we have emotional energy, when we are emotionally resilient, we can confront our problems with a sense of hope and power. When our emotional reserves are depleted, we are seriously weakened, out of perspective. Our strength is sapped, our resolve paralyzed, and we become even more emotionally vulnerable, which opens the door for more emotional energy depletion.

■ **Take care of your body.** It will be much more likely to be ready when you need it. When we don't take care of ourselves physically—underresting, underexercising, and overeating— we feel consistently tired and overwhelmed. We must be students of our bodies and work in harmony with them.

■ **Take time to play.** We need to have fun: personal time, time with family, fun with friends. According to a Harris Survey, the amount of leisure time enjoyed by the average American has decreased 37 percent since 1973. Over the same period, the average workweek, including commuting, has jumped from under forty-one hours to nearly forty-seven hours. It's important to balance heavy issues with lighter ones.

■ **Be a lifelong learner.** If you're feeling like an old dog, teach yourself some new tricks. Stimulating your mind with new information—via classes, books, apprenticeships—keeps it percolating with ideas and problem-solving abilities. Doing the opposite— thinking about the same things all the time, allowing your mind to go stale and empty of ideas—means you'll become boring and predictable, and so will your life.

■ **Develop your spiritual side.** Everyone has one. Deep down we all know we are more than the body we inhabit. Our souls need attention, too, al-

> In a lifetime, the average American will . . .
>
> Spend six months sitting at traffic lights, waiting for them to change.
>
> Spend one year searching through desk clutter for misplaced objects.
>
> Spend eight months opening junk mail.
>
> Spend two years trying to call people who aren't in or whose line is busy.
>
> Spend five years waiting in lines.
>
> Spend three years in meetings.
>
> Learn how to operate twenty thousand different things, from drink machines to can openers to digital radio controls.
>
> Be interrupted seventy-three times every day.
>
> Receive six hundred advertising messages every day (television, newspapers, magazines, radio, billboards).
>
> Watch seventeen hundred hours of television every year.
>
> Open six hundred pieces of mail every year.
>
> If we do all that, surely we have time to have fun.

though that's not always easily apparent. If I couldn't draw on God's strength and wisdom daily, I'm sure I'd collapse. I simply don't have all it takes to run my life and two careers by myself.

Top Ten Reasons Women Don't Take Care of Themselves

■ **Circumstances.** We live under the tyranny of the urgent: Whatever or whoever is screaming the loudest gets the attention—and something or someone is always making noise. One friend calls this "managing by fire"—she deals with whatever is making the most smoke at any given moment.

■ **Others' expectations.** We're all prone to succumb to the agendas of others. Granted, a six-month-old with a soggy diaper doesn't know he's got expectations and is exerting pressure on us, and his requests are reasonable! But sometimes we allow ourselves to be raw material for someone else's intentions. When is the last time you said yes to a request simply because some domineering person asked it of you?

■ **Natural boundaries.** We simply can't do all there is to do with the limited number of hours and amount of energy we have each day. We must make choices that reflect an understanding of this.

■ **Lack of focus.** If we don't examine our situation once in a while, we're never sure what we want or need to be doing because we haven't stopped long enough to figure it out.

■ **Love of comfort.** We all tend to avoid change, if possible. We want few surprises and a minimum of inconvenience, which change always brings, so we avoid the new in favor of the familiar. Consequently, we miss out on the good change often generates.

■ **Not enough time.** Actually we do have the time, it's just what we choose to spend it on.

■ **Fear of failure.** Safety has a friendly face, but it's deceptive. Sometimes the kindest and best thing we can do for ourselves, and those we love, is to take a risk.

■ **Misunderstanding the process.** We guess that taking control of our life so we can build in time for self-care is something we can initiate one day and master the next. The truth is, like any habit or change in lifestyle, it isn't an overnight occurrence.

■ **Lack of connection with the big picture.** When our eyes are fixed on getting through just this hour or this day, there's no way we can begin to plan for next week.

> "You can be pleased with nothing when you are not pleased with yourself."
> —Lady Mary Wortley Montagu

■ **Pride.** Sometimes we are simply unwilling to admit our need for change or help.

Making Self-Care a Habit

Whatever the circumstances in your life, there are always changes you can make and actions you can take that will help you build important self-care habits into your life.

■ **Create buffer zones in your schedule.** If you're flying from Seattle to Tampa via Dallas, the airlines will always allow more than three minutes to change planes in Dallas. Passengers need a much greater margin of error. We would do well to do this in our lives. If you have a busy schedule with nonstop appointments, create small buffer zones between them. Even ten minutes extra can defuse your tension.

■ **Collect people who inspire you.** All of us have people in our lives who drain us and others who replenish us. Make it a priority to seek out and spend time regularly with people you enjoy.

■ **Carve out some time to help others.** I know, I know: You already feel overloaded from helping those who depend on you. But I'm talking about a different kind of giving. Volunteer your time and talents at a soup kitchen, hospital, or homeless shelter. Their stresses will help you put yours in proportion, and you'll find that life takes on a new hue when you have a thankful heart.

- **Be smart about your monthly cycle.** Keep a calendar of emotions for a month or two. See if you can pinpoint when you're likely to be dealing with PMS, and be careful about what you schedule during that time. Don't volunteer to chaperone a junior-high retreat if you know your hormones will be wacky. When you're experiencing PMS, do whatever it takes to get plenty of rest, don't eat sweets, exercise as much as possible, and cut back on caffeine.

- **Spend some time each day outdoors.** Breathe some fresh air and feel the sunshine. Exercise outdoors, eat lunch outdoors, take weekend trips outdoors, sit by a sunny window, or read a book on your porch, even if it's only for ten to fifteen minutes at a time.

- **Look your best for yourself.** Getting into the rut of being sloppy in your appearance can drag you down and add to your stress. If I find myself sinking into a negative mood, I take a fragrant bubble bath, wash and style my hair, and put on a pretty outfit. It makes me feel better when I like what I see in the mirror.

> "I read and walked for miles at night along the beach, writing bad blank verse and searching endlessly for someone wonderful who would step out of the darkness and change my life. It never crossed my mind that that person could be me."
> —Anna Quindlen

- **Start working on a project or putter at a hobby you enjoy.** You do this for your kids, right? Give yourself the freedom to do things that are creative, too.

- **Find a special place that refreshes and inspires you,** whether it's a park bench, a mountain trail, the beach, or the woods. Make time to go there as a brief retreat to get away from the craziness of life and read or reflect. Trade baby-sitting with a friend who would like to do the same.

- **Schedule a "quiet time" every day and say no to interruptions.** Most women unconsciously and automatically put the needs of others—spouse, kids, friends—before their own. Our sleep, phone calls, meals, and even bathroom time are all fair game. We can provide some essential self-care by establishing a set quiet time each day—for example, between 2:30 and 3 P.M.—during which no one can ask for anything, barring an emergency. If you retreat to the bathroom to soak in the tub, put a Do Not Disturb sign on the door. Young children who don't take naps can be taught that even if they don't go to sleep, they must have quiet time in their rooms, looking at books, listening to tapes quietly, or playing with quiet toys. A mom who works outside the home told me that after dinner she gets her kids involved in homework or a project while she takes a bubble bath and reads a chapter in a novel for fifteen minutes. Everyone knows this is Mom's time, and although it's only fifteen minutes, she says the benefits to her and her family are many.

■ **Plan ahead for times of extra stress,** such as the holiday season or before a big project you're in charge of.

Sleep a little extra ahead of time.
Cut back on any activities you can.
Be sure you do your morning quiet time/meditation faithfully.
Eat wisely and don't skip vitamin and water-drinking regimens.
Plan your time as efficiently as possible.
Restrict the demands others impose on you.
Don't add anything unnecessary to your schedule. Wait until the crunch is over to get your teeth cleaned, for example.

■ **Stick to your priorities.** Taking time to care for yourself must be high on your list of what's important. Delete activities and commitments that are not fulfilling. Don't let other people "guilt" you into saying yes to things

---

Home-Front Reentry Time

Establish effective transition behaviors between your various roles and responsibilities. It usually takes about fifteen to twenty minutes to move, mentally and emotionally, from a stressful day of business to relaxation or refreshing recreation. At our house we call this "reentry time." Here are a few ideas:

■ Listen to soothing music or inspirational audiotapes on the drive home from work.

■ Take a catnap.

■ Take off your work uniform.

■ Put on a play uniform (tennis clothes, sweat suit, beach clothes).

■ Engage in a short exercise routine.

■ Spend twenty minutes in prayer or inspirational reading.

■ Have a chat with a friend you enjoy.

■ Walk your pet.

■ Work in your garden.

■ Play a musical instrument.

■ Read a novel.

■ Peruse a favorite magazine or catalog.

■ Resolve not to discuss work with your spouse for one hour after you get home.

that aren't priorities to you. Don't feel guilty about not doing what everyone wants you to do. Remember, when you say yes to something, you're saying no to something else. Don't let it be yourself.

■ **Learn to relax.** Consciously relax your brow. Drop your lower jaw. Avoid clenching your fists or holding tightly to objects; consciously relax your hands, especially when holding a pen, driving a car, or watching TV. Relax your stomach muscles. Breathe deeply.

■ **Count your blessings.** Make a list of the little blessings in your life from just last week. If none come to mind, answer some questions: Has your car been running smoothly? Do you have hot water for a shower? Has someone told you that he or she cares? Do you have clothes to wear? Has a co-worker complimented you? Is your roof not leaking? If it is, is it leaking in only three spots? Have you been able to make progress on a project? Has your child come home with a good grade? Attitude colors everything in our lives. Choosing to look for the good instead of focusing on what's bad or missing will make a huge difference in your ability to be happy and enjoy life.

■ **Plan for free time.** Block it out on your calendar just as you would an important appointment.

■ **Start an informal "support group."** Seek out like women and agree to be there for each other when life gets tough.

■ **Create a morning ritual.** Begin each day with something that inspires or energizes you, like reading over a cup of hot coffee, journaling, exercising, or listening to music. For years, I've had a morning ritual of getting up early and going to the Y to work out. I listen to inspirational music on the way there and back. When I come home, I read a portion of the Bible and pray for my family and friends and the coming events of the day. This prepares me to meet the challenges of the day ahead.

■ **Exercise.** When we exercise, our bodies produce endorphins, morphinelike substances that can deliver a feeling of peacefulness. Endorphins are the body's natural painkillers. Exercise also serves as an outlet for pent-up stress that frustrations and troublesome thoughts cause.

■ **Give someone else a mental and emotional lift.** Showing appreciation and praising someone else is a good way to lift your own spirits.

■ **Take a vacation.** Whether it's a getaway with your husband or a fun group of girlfriends, put this high on your list. But it's important to realize that a vacation can be just as stressful as what you left back home if you don't follow some simple rules. Here are some tips for how to take a *relaxing, refreshing* vacation:

> *Have realistic expectations.* A vacation won't change your life in a week, but it can and will be refreshing if you let it be.
>
> *Evaluate past vacations.* Without raking yourself or anyone else over the coals, think of what could be improved.
>
> *Give yourself permission to relax.* Don't fall prey to free-floating guilt that says you should be working or doing something more useful and that you shouldn't be having such a good time.
>
> *Laugh at obstacles and mishaps.* Don't let things like long lines and flat tires flatten your fun.
>
> *Decide on a vacation eating plan.* Overeating can ruin a vacation. Resistance is usually a little lower during vacations. Fatigue, frustration, and even boredom can stimulate indulgence.
>
> *Get regular exercise on your trip.* Aim for a good balance between rest and activity.

■ **Take a vacation from *something*.** If you can't take a vacation *to* someplace, taking a vacation *from* something can be restoring, even if it's only for twenty-four hours. For example, as a family or in your office, decide that you're going to take a vacation from complaining or making any negative comments for twenty-four hours. A vacation from television and radio can help clear your mind. A vacation from the phone also helps.

Taking Care of Your Body

Making fitness a priority isn't just about looking great. It's about caring for your one and only body in a way that promotes and increases health, energy, and longevity. Fitness also builds stamina. You can more easily go with less sleep for brief periods, your body bounces back from minor illnesses more quickly, you set a great lifelong example for your kids, you feel better about yourself, and you can cope with the inevitable setbacks of life more easily. In this section, you'll learn some simple ways to be healthy and feel your best.

"The first wealth is health."
—**Ralph Waldo Emerson**

Twenty-Two Good Reasons to Exercise

Regular exercise:

- Builds strong muscles and bones.

- Strengthens your heart.

- Reduces your risk of chronic diseases, including heart disease, osteoporosis, and high blood pressure.

- Helps control your weight.

- Reduces your risk of many types of cancers.

- Slows the aging process.

- Reduces symptoms of PMS.

- Relieves menstrual pain.

- Improves your self-image.

- Relieves depression.

- Improves the quality of your sleep.

- Improves your posture.

- Improves the quality of your life, particularly as you age.

Walking is the easiest exercise to start. It strengthens your body and relaxes your mind. It requires no expensive equipment (only a good pair of walking shoes), no training, and no expensive facilities.

- Increases your metabolism and decreases your appetite.

- Releases stress.

- Reduces the severity of varicose veins.

- Gives you more energy.

- Increases your resistance to fatigue.

- Helps you be more productive at work.

- Builds stamina for other physical activities.

- Increases your feeling of well-being.

- You're setting a good example for your children.

> If you haven't been involved in an exercise program for a long time, particularly if you're over forty or overweight, consult your doctor before beginning. Remember, exercise doesn't have to be expensive or fancy. You don't need a large wardrobe, state-of-the-art equipment, or a membership in an exclusive gym.

Put Muscle into Your Day

Researchers at the University of Vermont in Burlington recently found that a flagging metabolism is not an inevitable part of aging. It's due primarily to a loss of muscle mass. After the mid-twenties, an average adult loses a half-pound of muscle every year. The best way to add muscle mass is through weight training. You can use health-club weight machines, take a weight-training class, or work out at home with a set of free weights, about three to five pounds each. Besides these general benefits, weight training and other exercise can increase your resting metabolic rate by as much as 5 to 10 percent for several hours afterward, sparking what is known as the afterburn effect. After two months, you'll add enough muscle to burn about 108 additional calories each day. For specific exercises, consult a fitness professional or another reliable source.

Twenty-four Simple Ways to Sneak Exercise into Your Life

- Turn the playground into a gym and get fit while your tot is busy having fun. Work the equipment. Giving your child a ride on the merry-go-round will rev up your heart, firm up your arms, and strengthen your legs. Pushing her on a swing is also great for toning your arms. You can also grab a pole and do some leg lifts while she's playing in the sandbox.

- Park at a far-off parking spot and take the opportunity to walk when you're running errands.

- Invest in an exercise video and work out at home.

- Don't sit to chat with a friend; schedule a time to walk and talk instead.

- Get off the bus before your stop and walk the rest of the way.

- Schedule active fun for weekends: hiking, bowling, tennis, swimming.

- Take the stairs instead of the elevator.

- While drying your hair, do some leg lunges.

- Store a pair of athletic shoes at the office so you can take advantage of a sunny lunch hour.

- While watching TV, do some crunches.

- If you don't have blocks of time available, do brief stints of exercise instead: three ten-minute activities instead of thirty continuous minutes.

- While you drive, tighten your thighs, buttocks, and tummy.

- Pick up a two- or three-pound weight and work your biceps while you chat on the phone.

- Wash your car yourself.

- If you use a health club or gym, join one close to your office or home.

- When working at the kitchen counter, do calf raises.

- Make those waits work: Walk in the hall by the doctor's office until he or she is ready for you; stroll around the block if you're told there's a thirty-minute wait for a table at a restaurant.

- When your kids go skating, go with them.

- Swing your arms when you walk.

■ Play tag with the kids.

■ Do leg lifts while dinner is cooking.

■ Wear weights on each ankle while puttering around the house: walking to and from the laundry room, getting the mail, putting towels away upstairs.

■ Do housework briskly.

■ Go ahead—swim, walk, dance, skate—now, not twenty pounds from now.

Tips for Sticking with It

■ List reasons you might skip exercise. Recognize them when you're tempted to put off exercising.

■ Think of a way to reward yourself for every exercise appointment you keep.

■ Make yourself accountable to someone who's allowed to remind you to exercise.

■ Schedule exercise time with friends.

■ If you work out alone, play some music.

■ Put your gym clothes by the door as a reminder to go exercise at lunchtime.

■ Choose a workout center close to your home or office.

■ Exercise at home—you won't have bad weather as an excuse.

■ To avoid boredom, do a variety of exercises: jogging, water fitness, strength training.

■ Don't overdo. If you pull a muscle, you might get so discouraged that you quit altogether.

■ Remember to warm up and cool down—don't just jump into strenuous exercise.

■ If you miss a day, just get back to it as soon as you can. Berating yourself does more harm than good.

Consider joining a weight-loss program or going to a self-help support group. It's easier to maintain changes in our lives when we have support. Check the Yellow Pages for a program near you. Churches, neighborhood centers, Ys, and other community-based organizations often offer such support groups.

- Keep a journal that lists days you exercised and what you did.

- Get rid of your bathroom scale. Determine your fitness by how you feel instead.

- Expect to succeed. Positive thinking does wonders.

- Encourage yourself with kind words: "You did it! Good job!"

- Give yourself credit for being in the process of becoming healthy and fit!

Lifelong Healthy Eating Habits

Small changes can make a huge difference in our health and well-being. Here are some simple ways to get on the road to a better you.

SHOPPING

- Don't buy foods that tempt you. If you know you "can't eat just one," leave them at the store!

- Never shop for groceries on an empty stomach. You'll be less likely to yield to tempting displays.

- Become a label reader. Avoid refined sugar and high-carbohydrate foods.

- Stock up on healthy foods that are ready to eat or quickly and easily prepared.

COOKING

- Allow soups and stews to chill after cooking so you can see the fat and skim it off.

- Switch to low- and nonfat dairy products. Many taste as good as high-fat products.

■ Use fat-burning spices. A British study showed that adding hot chili sauce and spicy yellow mustard to a meal increased study subjects' metabolism up to 25 percent for the next three hours. A mere ⅗ teaspoon can do the trick.

■ Substitute applesauce for oil in baked products. (Applesauce contains pectin, which helps maintain a moist texture. However, if the recipe's only liquid is oil, you might need to use half applesauce and half nonfat milk to ensure moistness.)

■ Use cholesterol-free egg substitutes or egg whites instead of whole eggs in any recipe. (Substitute two egg whites for one whole egg.)

■ Substitute nonfat plain yogurt for sour cream when baking. Or place one 16-ounce carton of nonfat cottage cheese in a blender with 2 tablespoons nonfat yogurt and 2 tablespoons lemon juice. Blend until smooth and use instead of sour cream.

■ When sautéing, use wine, nonfat cooking spray, or chicken broth instead of oil.

■ Bake, broil, or roast instead of frying.

■ Allow yourself only three taste samples of whatever you're cooking.

Five Reasons Not to Go on a Crash Diet

Weight loss is a $4-billion-dollar-a-year business. According to a report from the Centers for Disease Control and Prevention, on any given day, half of American women are dieting. Before you begin another fad diet, consider these facts:

■ The only diet that works is the one you can stick with for the rest of your life.

■ When you drastically reduce the calories you consume, instead of losing fat cells, you encourage the loss of muscle cells that burn fat.

■ When you crash diet, you rob your body of the energy it needs to burn fat correctly—through more physical activity. If we want to burn fat, we have to take in enough quality calories to give our bodies the energy to do fat-burning exercise.

■ Extreme dieting actually lowers the rate at which your body burns calories. If you feed your body only 500 calories a day, it automatically goes into starvation mode and burns calories at a much slower rate than usual. On the other hand, exercise does exactly the opposite. It sets into motion bio-chemical changes that speed up calorie-burning.

■ Changing your *lifestyle*—changing the way you eat in healthy, positive ways so you feel and look your best for the rest of your life—is the only way to control your weight.

Determine how much water you need each day by dividing your weight in two. This gives you the total number of ounces. Divide that amount by eight to determine how many glasses. So for example, if you weigh 140 pounds, you should drink 70 ounces of water a day. Seventy divided by 8 equals 8.75. So you should be drinking about nine 8-ounce glasses of water a day.

EATING AND DRINKING

■ Eat when you are hungry. Stop when you are full.

■ Don't mistake thirst for hunger. Occasionally, you might crave something cold such as ice cream when all you really want is something to drink. Next time you get such a craving, have water first and see if it goes away.

■ Leave serving bowls in the kitchen during meals, so you'll have to reconsider and walk to get seconds.

■ Brush your teeth after meals to avoid the temptation to keep eating.

■ Never eat standing up.

■ Put less food on your fork or spoon, and take smaller bites.

■ Always put salad dressing on the side.

■ Even if you eat alone, don't watch TV or read while you eat. I'm usually all in favor of multitasking, but eating is not exactly a task. We tend to pay too little attention to what we eat anyway. It's too easy to keep eating long after we're full if we're engrossed in a book or a TV program.

■ Be an early bird eater. Your body burns calories most efficiently during the first twelve hours of the day. So eat at least 25 percent of your calories at breakfast and the same at lunch. Don't eat anything after 8 o'clock in the evening.

■ Eat slowly and play calm background music while you eat. Research shows we eat faster when we listen to fast music while eating.

■ Don't assume healthy eating means torturing yourself with foods you dislike day after day. Instead, find good-food choices you enjoy.

"Health is the thing that makes you feel that now is the best time of year." —Franklin P. Adams

■ Allow yourself small portions of favorite foods each day.

■ Pack your own snacks when you're traveling.

Sleep: You Can't Function Without It

Only you can know your own body and how much rest you need. Some women can't function without seven or eight hours of sleep. Some do fine on five or six. The amount of sleep we need is related to how soundly we sleep, how hard we are working, and what other ways we find to rest between sleep periods. Diet and exercise also directly affect both quantity and quality of sleep. Instead of worrying about whether the amount you sleep is "right," ask yourself what percentage of the time you feel adequately rested. Studies have shown that doing daily aerobic exercise can decrease the amount of sleep people require. Exercise provides some of the benefits of sleep in that it helps to release tension and stress toxins, thereby producing a feeling of relaxation and well-being. It also tends to produce deeper and less-fitful sleep. We must all be students of our bodies and work in harmony with them. Also, it's important to remember that illness, heavy workloads, sadness, and stress can increase the amount of sleep your body needs.

"The more naps you take, the more awakenings you experience."
—Sarah Ban Breathnach

If you have consistent difficulty sleeping, here are some ideas:

- Start a sleep routine. Read, listen to music, pray with your child, etc. This prepares you to hit the hay.

- Write a detailed to-do list for the next day—and then forget about it.

- If your bed or pillow is uncomfortable, replace it.

- Don't do office work or balance your checkbook in the bedroom. Train yourself to see it as a place to rest and relax.

- Some doctors recommend the use of herbs such as valerian root. Check with your physician before trying any herbal treatment.

- Take a long, hot soak in the tub before bed. This starts the relaxation process.

"Finish every day and be done with it. You have done what you could. Some blunders and absurdities no doubt crept in; forget them as soon as you can. Tomorrow is a new day. Begin it well." **—Ralph Waldo Emerson**

De-Stress Yourself

Stress is the reaction we have when small irritations or big catastrophes enter our lives. When we have too much stress for too long, it can result in such physical damage as high-blood pressure, a weak immune system, ulcers, headaches, heart disease, and arthritis, among others. Our bodies give us clear warning signs when we're nearing stress overload. Little things that once didn't phase us now set us off. We might have trouble relaxing or feel like a human pressure cooker—always ready to blow our top.

We all have hidden stressors in our lives, and identifying them is the first step to eliminating them. Go through the following list and ask yourself if any of these things are giving you a stress signal:

- [ ] Cartoons blaring from the family TV
- [ ] Your teenager's stereo system
- [ ] Living near a noisy freeway, railroad, or airport
- [ ] Bad lighting
- [ ] An uncomfortable desk chair
- [ ] Dogs barking
- [ ] Violence on the evening news
- [ ] A drawer that comes off the track every time you open it
- [ ] Clutter
- [ ] A never-diminishing pile of ironing
- [ ] The mail
- [ ] Ill-fitting clothes
- [ ] Uncomfortable shoes
- [ ] A spouse who won't talk
- [ ] Remodeling or construction
- [ ] A messy house
- [ ] A decrease in pay or increase in hours
- [ ] Problems with your car
- [ ] Difficulty sleeping
- [ ] Illness in family
- [ ] Houseguests
- [ ] Debt
- [ ] Sexual difficulty
- [ ] Anger toward your spouse
- [ ] Anger toward your children
- [ ] Trouble with in-laws
- [ ] Weather conditions

If you feel near—or past—the boiling point, consider consulting a counselor. Give yourself the freedom to treat stress as you would any other chronic condition. If you had persistent back pain, you'd seek a doctor and get treatment. Pain like this—personal, relational, and situational stress—deserves the same focused attention.

Turn Energy Zappers into Energy Boosters

The bionic woman is a fictional character. Although your daily workload might seem like a superhuman job, your body is only human and must be cared for as such. If you're feeling tired all the time, chances are one or more of these habits are to blame. The good news—it's easy to make a small lifestyle change to turn these zappers into energy boosters.

Quench thirst. You lose the equivalent of ten cups of water from everyday living. And you replace only about four through eating. Hidden dehydration robs you of energy and makes you feel lethargic. Drink water all day, every day.

Eat wisely. Have you ever finished a meal and wanted to go lie down? It might be because you fed your body high-fat foods, which tend to make us lethargic. Eat low-fat, low-carb foods and balanced meals to avoid the desire to nap. And remember, protein is brain food—and who couldn't use a little more brain power?

Get enough rest. If you don't sleep consistently at the same time for at least seven to eight hours, you are probably throwing your body out of whack. Inconsistent sleep patterns will leave you lethargic. Sleep isn't an indulgence; it's a necessity.

Let there be light. When it's dark, your body says "Sleep." When it's light, your body says "Get up and move!" When you get up in the morning, throw open the curtains immediately. Get as much light as you can, and you'll feel more energetic.

Turn off the TV. When you feed your mind with television, you are encouraging your body to be passive. Even "smart" shows such as the evening news can zap energy because they put your body into sedentary mode. So take television

> "To put the world in order, we must first put the nation in order; to put the nation in order, we must put the family in order; to put the family in order, we must cultivate our personal life; and to cultivate our personal life, we must first set our hearts right." —Confucius

in moderation, and be sure you're being active the rest of the time. Make activity, not TV, the highlight of your day. And keep an exercise mat nearby, so that when you do watch TV, you can get in some exercise at the same time.

Take vitamins. Ask your physician for what's right for you. At the very least, you should take a multivitamin. Be good to your body so it will be good to you.

Developing Your Spiritual Self

Many people live with a conviction that they are more than they appear. If you believe that each person is also created with a spiritual side, you have a special wellspring from which to draw in tough times. Let's face it: None of us has a perfect life. We all deal with sickness, pain, loneliness, disappointment, insecurity, failure, and death. Often, how we face the storms of trouble in our lives, and how they affect us for the rest of our lives, depends on our faith and spirituality.

As with our body and mind, our spiritual development is never a done deal. There are endless possibilities and untapped potential to be revealed in all of us. Whatever your faith, it should cover the serious issues of life:

- Does your faith give your life meaning, purpose, and peace?

- Does your faith support you in every phase of living: adolescence, young adulthood, middle age, old age, marriage crises, financial crises, children's crises, energy crises, cultural crises, and moral crises?

- Does it deal with guilt and forgiveness?

- Does it answer the question of evil and still give you hope?

- Does it provide a way for you to look realistically at the problems of life without despair?

Set aside some time to think about spiritual issues and their relevance in your life. Be honest about your questions and doubts as you search for answers.

Here are ways to develop your spiritual self in ways that make you stronger, happier, and more at peace:

- Seek to be an authentic person—what you say you believe is reflected in how you live your life.

- When you face a dilemma, say to God, "If you are who you say you are, please give me guidance and help." After you ask, be quiet and listen with your heart and mind. He promised, "Call to me and I will answer you and tell you great and unsearchable things you do not know." (Jeremiah 33:3)

- Read a portion of the Bible every day. Underline passages that speak to you.

- When you read a book by an author who inspires to you, try to read more of his or her writings.

- Spend time with spiritual people you admire. Learn from them.

- Jot down ideas, prayers, verses, and quotes from books that give you insight and wisdom.

- If you have the question in your mind, "How do I know there is a God?" perhaps a more pertinent question would be, "If there *is* in fact a God, how can I find him?"

- Practice Sabbath rest. Someone once said, "God rested—and He wasn't tired." Rest is an opportunity for contemplation, reflection, and remembering what's at the center of the universe.

- Collect inspirational music—music is the language of the soul.

- Try to watch at least one sunrise or sunset each week.

- Remind yourself to be conscious of God's presence—in quiet moments at home, or in sleepless moments in the middle of the night.

- Take a walk in the park with a small child, adopting his or her sense of wonder. See what the child sees, and give yourself permission to express the same awe of nature.

- Start the day by reading from a devotional book such as *My Utmost for His Highest* by Oswald Chambers.

- When you eat something today, really taste it—and be thankful for the taste buds that let you enjoy it.

- Consider these words of Francis Bacon and celebrate the unfathomable complexities of the world: "A little science estranges a man from God. A lot of science brings him back."

- In a difficult situation, look for at least one thing you can be grateful for.

- Write a thank you note to someone who has had a positive impact on your life.

- Practice spontaneous gratitude. When something positive happens to you or someone you love, pause and thank God.

- Give thanks before meals. Thank God for all the people who worked to get it on your table—the farmer, the trucker, the grocer.

- When you get into an ungrateful state of mind and begin to gripe and complain, try to see yourself in the future—how you'll want to have responded to the situation.

- Celebrate something good that happens to you by doing something good for someone else. You'll find your joy is doubled.

- Keep a prayer journal. Write down your requests and record the answers. This will help you clarify your thoughts, be alert to answered prayers, and build your awareness of God at work in your life.

- Make a list of the ways you've fallen short and want to feel forgiven. Turn what you write down into a prayer of confession and thanksgiving for forgiveness. Use the Psalms to help you express your feelings to God.

- When you act in a way that is hurtful to yourself or others, ask forgiveness—from the other person and from God.

- Forgive others in your life as you would like to be forgiven.

- Share spiritual ideas with a friend. We can deepen our spiritual lives both by hearing others' beliefs and by saying our own out loud.

"No man is poor who has a godly mother." —Abraham Lincoln

- Join a Bible study or small group with other people who want to grow spiritually.

- Worship regularly.

- Take time to reflect on important spiritual ideas—the ones you want your life to emulate. As you turn them over in your mind, you'll find yourself living out the principles that have become a part of you.

- Take the time to get to know an older person whose spirituality you respect, who might be lonely and has a lot to teach.

- Make growing spiritually a lifelong process. Author Madeleine L'Engle said, "I do not think that I will ever reach a stage when I will say, 'This is what I believe. Finished.' What I believe is alive . . . and open to growth."

"The ordinary arts we practice every day at home are of more importance to the soul than their simplicity might suggest."
—Thomas Moore

Everyday Acts of Spirituality

- Practice self-control—let your husband wear his ratty sweatshirt in peace.

- Tell your son or daughter, "I'm thankful for the privilege of being your mother."

- Listen to family members with your eyes as well as with your ears.

- Hug your moody teenager.

- Offer to help someone who crosses your path today in a practical way.

- If you offend your spouse or child, say you're sorry—sincerely.

- Plan extra spots at your family's holiday table, and fill them with people who would otherwise be left alone.

- Volunteer to do someone else's chore for them, even though it's not your turn.

- Call your mother-in-law. Tell her how much you appreciate your husband.

- Say something encouraging to somcone at least once a day.

"Our souls are hungry for meaning, for the sense that we have figured out how to live so that our lives matter, so that the world will be at least a little bit different for our having passed throught it.."
—Harold Kushner

Kathy Peel is founder and president of Family Manager Inc., a company that provides helpful resources to strengthen busy families and help make home a great place to be.

Visit www.familymanager.com to:

- Inquire about Kathy speaking to your group or organization.

- Read about Kathy's upcoming media appearances.

- Find out how to become a Family Manager Consultant.

- Download free forms mentioned in this book.

- Learn about more helpful products and resources from Family Manager.

Index